*Colonial
Williamsburg
Decorates for
Christmas*

Visitors to Williamsburg always admire the simple yet elegant boxwood wreath with pomegranates on the gate of the Governor's Palace. Instructions for making this wreath are given on page 24.

Colonial Williamsburg Decorates for Christmas

Step-by-step illustrated instructions for Christmas Decorations that you can make for your home

By Libbey Hodges Oliver, *Supervisor, Flower Section, Colonial Williamsburg*
  and
Betty Hundley Babb, Elizabeth Mack Booth, Betsy Kent, and Martha Marquardt

Photographs by
  Frank J. Davis and Dan Spangler

Line Drawings by
  Louis Luedtke

Published by
The Colonial Williamsburg Foundation
Williamsburg, Virginia

Library of Congress Cataloging in Publication Data

Oliver, Libbey Hodges
    Colonial Williamsburg Decorates for Christmas

    1. Christmas decorations — Virginia — Williamsburg.
    I. Colonial Williamsburg Foundation.
    II. Title.

TT900.C4037   745.92   81-10103
ISBN 0-87935-056-3   AACR2
ISBN 0-87935-058-X (pbk.)

Printed in the United States of America

Contents

Introduction 7

Wreaths and Other Outdoor Decorations

Basic Boxwood Wreath 10

Boxwood and White Pine Wreath 12

Double-Faced Boxwood Wreath 13

Boxwood on Straw Base Wreath 16

Wreath of Apples and Holly Berries 17

Wreath of Lemons and Limes 18

Mixed Fruit Wreath 20

George Wythe House Matching Wreaths 22

Brush-Everard House Wreath of Lemons, Limes, and Natural

    Materials 23

Governor's Palace Pomegranate Wreath 24

Traditional Mixed Fruit Wreath 26

Pine Cone Flower Wreath 27

Plaque of Lady Apples and Pine Cones 28

Plaque Featuring Fruit and Natural Materials 30

James Geddy House Red Peppers Plaque 32

Apple Fan 34

Decoration for a Windowsill 36

Table Decorations

Mixed Fruit Curve with Nuts and Berries 40

Apple Cone 42

Mixed Fruit Cone 44

Osage Orange Cone 46

Lemon Cone 47

Brush-Everard House Table Decoration 48

Epergne 50

Table Decoration Featuring Oranges and Limes 52

Table Decoration Created for the Peyton Randolph House 53

Christmas Table at the George Wythe House 54

Accents

Holly Swag for Sconce 58

White Pine Swag for Sconce 59

Roping 60

Door Corner Accent of Holly Berries 61

Door Corner Accent of Lady Apples 62

Pomegranate Accent 63

Star Cluster of Cones 64

Cranberry Strings 65

Mantel Decoration of Fruit and Natural Materials 65

Mantel Arrangement Featuring Pineapple and Lemons 68

Decorations Featuring Herbs and Dried and Natural Materials

Dried Herb Wreath 70

Herb Kissing Ball 72

Table Decoration Designed for the Dining Room at Carter's Grove

    Plantation 73

Garland Designed for the Mantel at Carter's Grove Plantation 76

Pyramid of Herbs and Fresh Fruits 78

Introduction

EACH CHRISTMAS, the exhibition buildings, homes, and shops of Colonial Williamsburg are adorned with wreaths and garlands of natural materials for the holiday season. The flower arranging staff of the Colonial Williamsburg Foundation is responsible for creating exterior and interior decorations for all of the buildings in the Historic Area that are open to the public. Members of the staff also decorate Carter's Grove plantation on the James River and Bassett Hall, the former Williamsburg home of Mr. and Mrs. John D. Rockefeller, Jr., and their family. Private residences in the Historic Area of Virginia's eighteenth-century capital are decorated by the occupants.

Members of the flower arranging staff design and execute twenty-five elaborate exterior door wreaths and plaques every year, and they create elegant interior table and mantel arrangements for the exhibit rooms as well. More than two hundred plain white pine wreaths and nine hundred yards of white pine roping are used to put the finishing touch on doorways, windows, columns, and railings.

In addition to decorating the exhibition buildings, the flower arranging staff also conducts how-to workshops—in Williamsburg and elsewhere—at which they demonstrate how to make the decorations for which Colonial Williamsburg has become so famous.

The wreaths, cones, garlands, and other beautiful decorations constructed from natural materials have become associated with a Williamsburg-style Christmas and are so popular that we have received many requests for directions telling how to make them. This book, which contains detailed instructions for making forty-two different decorations, is being published by the Colonial Williamsburg Foundation so that our friends will be able to create their own decorations at home.

Before you begin to make any of the decorations in this book, it would be helpful to read the list of ingredients and the instructions first. The gauges, sizes, and numbers of floral wire and picks, fruit, and plant materials called for should be followed until you feel creative enough to improvise. For instance, it is difficult to wire a piece of fruit with floral wire lighter than the #16 gauge recommended. In the case of floral wire, the higher the gauge number, the lighter its weight. Floral pins are also known as greening pins or fern pins. Wire frames are used as the base for wreaths at Colonial Williamsburg because they enable the creation of thicker, longer lasting wreaths than do the easier to find straw bases. Clippers are needed for most of the decorations. If they are made with cutting edges that are kept sharp (not the anvil type), the decorations will be much easier to construct. Many of the decorations call for the same supplies, which are available from florists, craft shops, or garden centers, so it may be desirable to purchase them in bulk. After Christmas, the floral pins, picks, frames, and dried pods and cones can be saved for the next year.

The detailed instructions, helpful step-by-step drawings, and color closeups in this book will enable you to create a wide variety of decorations—from a basic wreath to a complicated cone; from a simple accent to an elaborate centerpiece for your table. Symmetry and elegance are the essence of each decoration. The dried arrangements, which may take a bit longer to construct, can be reused year after year.

Although detailed directions are given for each decoration, you should feel free to let your own creativity and skills help you develop adaptations and variations. Because available plant materials may vary from one area to another, a croton leaf might be substituted for an aucuba leaf or a rhododendron for a magnolia. It is more fun to work with berries, cones, and greens that are abundant and familiar. Be creative!

LIBBEY HODGES OLIVER

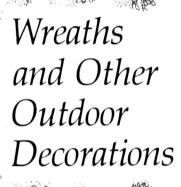

Wreaths
and Other
Outdoor
Decorations

Basic Boxwood Wreath

1 25-foot spool of #22 gauge wire
1 flat 2-wire wreath frame 18 inches in diameter
1 ½ bushels of 5-inch sprigs of boxwood
Wire cutters
Clippers

WRAP the end of the wire on the spool around the outer wire on the wreath frame several times to secure it. Do not cut the wire from the spool.①

Assemble a cluster of 6 sprigs of boxwood and lay it on the wreath frame.② Wrap the attached spool wire very tightly around the cut ends of the boxwood several times,③ then wrap the wire very tightly around the wreath frame several times.④ Do not cut the wire.

Assemble another cluster of 6 sprigs of box-wood the same size as the first. Lay it on the first cluster 1 to 2 inches down from the top of the foliage so that it overlaps the first cluster and covers the wired ends as illustrated.⑤ Wrap the attached spool wire very tightly around the cut ends of the second cluster and then around the wreath frame.⑥

Keep the clusters of boxwood uniform in size. To complete the wreath, continue wiring clusters of boxwood onto the frame, working in one direction.

Attach the last cluster of boxwood by lifting the first cluster up and wiring the last cluster under it.⑦ Wrap the attached spool wire tightly around the ends of the last cluster and then around the wreath frame. Leave 1 inch of wire to wrap around the frame. Cut the wire from the spool with the wire cutters and wrap the 1-inch end around the outer wire on the wreath frame several times to secure it. ⑧

Clip off any protruding pieces of foliage.

Attach a wire to the wreath frame for hanging.

NOTE: In Williamsburg, American and English boxwood are used for wreaths. Other readily available greens such as short-needled pines, balsam, hemlock, red cedar, arbor vitae, or Japanese holly may be substituted.

Boxwood and White Pine Wreath

1 25-foot spool of #22 gauge wire
1 flat 2-wire wreath frame 18 inches in diameter
¾ bushel of 5-inch sprigs of boxwood
¾ bushel of 5-inch sprigs of white pine
Wire cutters
Clippers

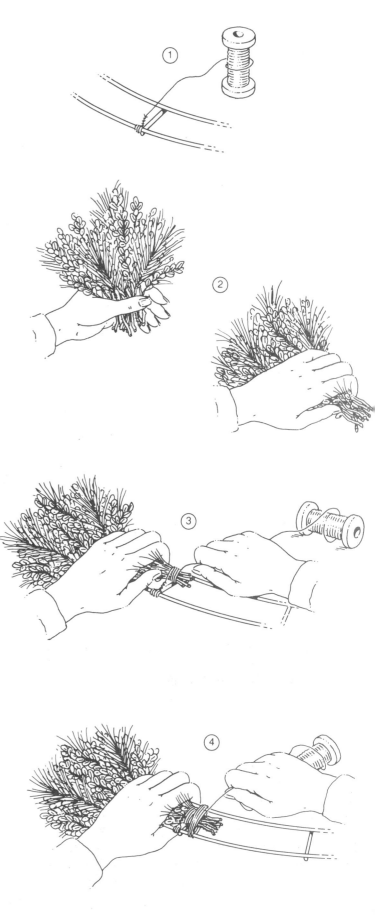

WRAP the end of the wire on the spool around the outer wire on the wreath frame several times to secure it. Do not cut the wire from the spool.①

Assemble a random mixed cluster of 3 to 4 sprigs of boxwood and 3 to 4 sprigs of white pine and lay it on the wreath frame.② Wrap the attached spool wire very tightly around the cut ends of the boxwood and white pine several times,③ then wrap the wire very tightly around the wreath frame several times.④ Do not cut the wire.

Assemble another random mixed cluster of 3 to 4 sprigs of boxwood and 3 to 4 sprigs of white pine the same size as the first. Lay it on the first cluster 1 to 2 inches down from the top of the foliage so that it overlaps the first cluster and covers the wired ends as illustrated.⑤ Wrap the attached spool wire very tightly around the cut ends of the second cluster and then around the wreath frame.⑥

Keep the random mixed clusters of boxwood and white pine uniform in size. To complete the wreath, continue wiring random mixed clusters of boxwood and white pine onto the frame, working in one direction.

Attach the last cluster of greens by lifting the first cluster up and wiring the last cluster under it.⑦ Wrap the attached spool wire tightly around the ends of the last cluster and then around the wreath frame. Leave 1 inch of wire to wrap around the frame. Cut the wire from the spool with the wire cutters and wrap the 1-inch end around the outer wire on the wreath frame several times to secure it. ⑧

Clip off any protruding pieces of foliage.

Attach a wire to the wreath frame for hanging.

NOTE: Other greens such as hemlock, holly with berries, red cedar, or arbor vitae may be used to make this wreath.

Double-Faced Boxwood Wreath

1 25-foot spool of #22 gauge wire
1 flat 2-wire wreath frame 18 inches in diameter
3 bushels of 5-inch sprigs of boxwood
Wire cutters
Clippers

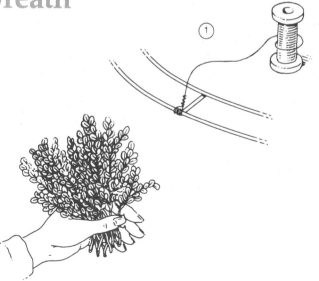

WRAP the end of the wire on the spool around the outer wire on the wreath frame several times to secure it. Do not cut the wire from the spool.①

Assemble a cluster of 6 sprigs of boxwood and lay it on the wreath frame.② Wrap the attached spool wire very tightly around the cut ends of the

Continued

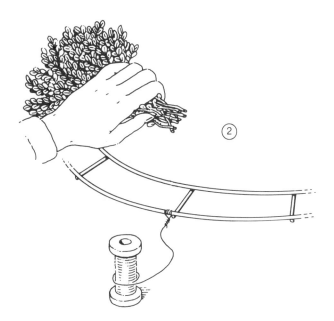

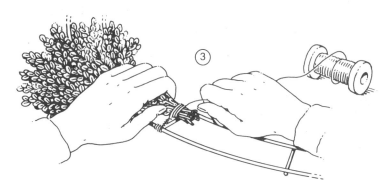

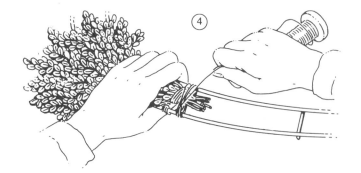

boxwood several times,③ then wrap the wire very tightly around the wreath frame several times.④ Do not cut the wire.

Turn the wreath over. Assemble a second cluster of 6 sprigs of boxwood and lay it on the wreath frame directly in back of the first attached cluster and in the same direction.⑤ Wrap the attached spool wire very tightly around the cut ends of the boxwood several times, then wrap the wire very tightly around the wreath frame several times.⑥

Assemble a third cluster of 6 sprigs of boxwood and lay it on the cluster just attached 1 to 2 inches down from the top of the foliage of the second cluster so that it overlaps the second cluster and covers the wired ends. Wrap the attached spool wire very tightly around the cut ends of the boxwood several times, then around the wreath frame several times.⑦

Turn the wreath over. Assemble a fourth cluster of 6 sprigs of boxwood and lay it on the first attached cluster on the first side of the wreath 1 to 2 inches down from the top of the foliage so that it overlaps the first attached cluster and covers the wired ends.⑧

Keep the clusters of boxwood uniform in size. To complete the wreath, continue wiring clusters of boxwood onto the frame, working in one direction. Attach 2 clusters of boxwood on 1 side of the wreath, then turn the wreath over and attach 2 more clusters. Proceed in this manner until the last cluster on each side is ready to be attached. Occasionally wrap the wire around the greens, working the wire down in and around the foliage on the other side so that it will be concealed. This will produce a tightly constructed wreath.

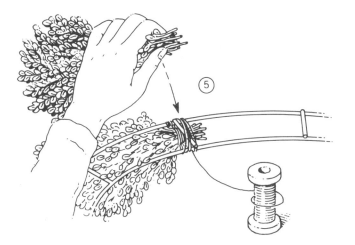

Attach the last cluster on each side by lifting the first cluster up and wiring the last cluster under it. ⑨ Wrap the attached spool wire around the ends of the last cluster on each side and then around the wreath frame. Leave 1 inch of wire to wrap around the frame. Cut the wire from the spool with the wire cutters and wrap the 1-inch end around the outer wire on the wreath frame several times to secure it. ⑩

Clip off any protruding pieces of foliage.

Attach a wire to the wreath frame for hanging.

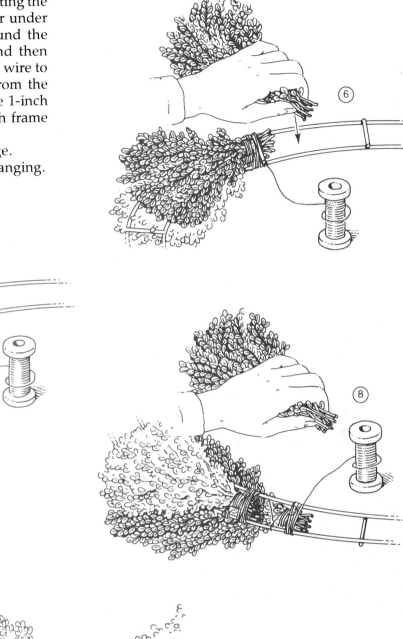

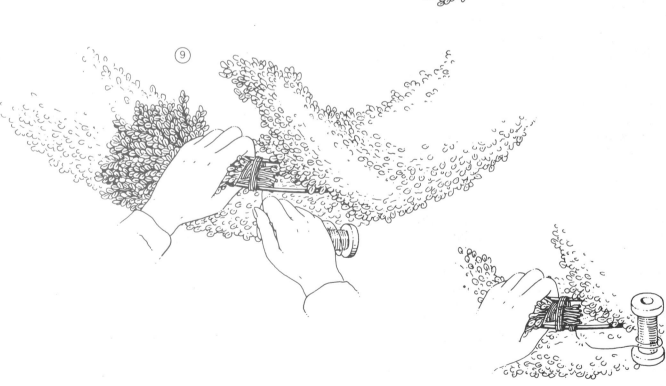

Boxwood on Straw Base Wreath

1 straw base wreath 18 inches in diameter wrapped
  in green plastic
Floral pins
1 bushel of 5-inch sprigs of boxwood
Clippers

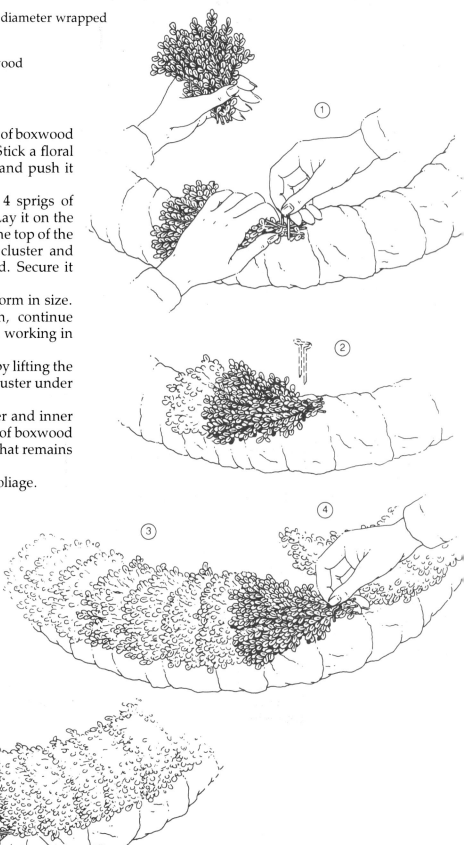

ASSEMBLE a cluster of 3 to 4 sprigs of boxwood
and lay it on top of the straw base. Stick a floral
pin over the stems of the boxwood and push it
in. ①

Assemble another cluster of 3 to 4 sprigs of
boxwood the same size as the first. Lay it on the
first cluster 1 to 2 inches down from the top of the
foliage so that it overlaps the first cluster and
covers the pinned ends as illustrated. Secure it
with a floral pin. ②

Keep the clusters of boxwood uniform in size.
To complete the top of the wreath, continue
pinning clusters onto the straw base, working in
one direction. ③

Attach the last cluster of boxwood by lifting the
first cluster up and pinning the last cluster under
it. ④

Repeat the same steps for the outer and inner
edges of the wreath. ⑤ Extra clusters of boxwood
may be required to cover any plastic that remains
exposed.

Clip off any protruding pieces of foliage.

NOTE: The floral pins will hold
best if the stems of the boxwood
are kept short and as non-woody
as possible. This wreath may be
double faced.

16

Wreath of Apples and Holly Berries

1 basic boxwood wreath constructed on an 18-inch
    wreath frame (page 10)
16 pieces of #16 gauge floral wire in 18-inch lengths
16 medium red Delicious apples
Wire cutters
3- to 4-inch sprigs of holly berries with the leaves
    removed

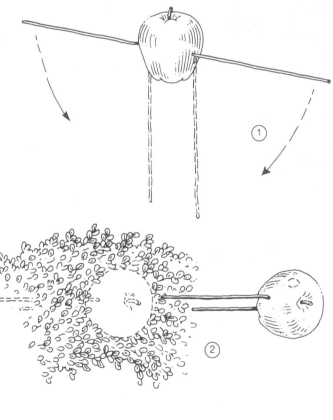

Push a piece of wire midway through the side
center of each apple so that it protrudes an equal
distance on each side of the apple. Bend the wires
into a "U" shape toward the base of each apple. ①

   Center an apple at the top of the wreath. Attach
the apple to the wreath by holding the wire ends 2
inches apart and pushing them through the middle of the boxwood.② Twist the wires several
times at the back of the wreath to secure the
apple.③ Cut off any excess wire.

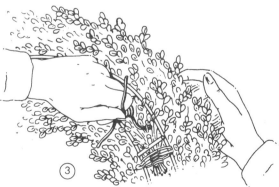

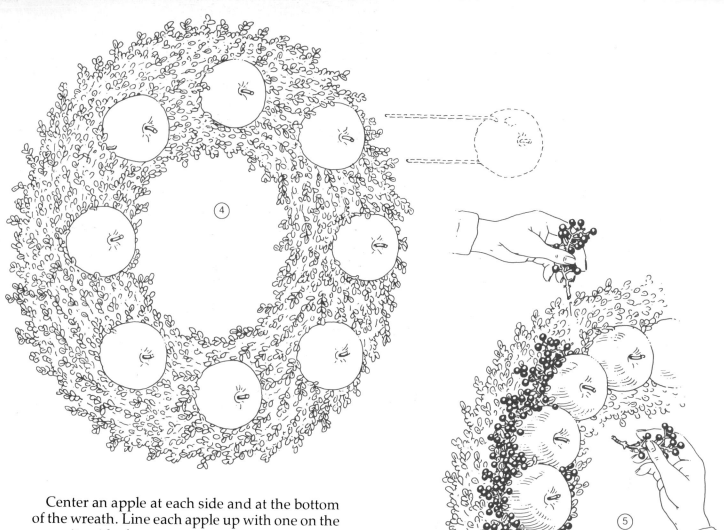

Center an apple at each side and at the bottom of the wreath. Line each apple up with one on the opposite side for a symmetrical design. Attach the remaining apples in the same manner.④

Tuck the sprigs of holly berries into the box-wood around the apples. ⑤

Wreath of Lemons and Limes

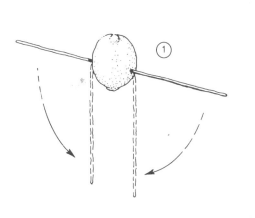

1 basic boxwood wreath constructed on a 20-inch wreath frame
32 pieces of #16 gauge floral wire in 18-inch lengths
16 medium lemons
16 medium limes
Wire cutters
4- to 6-inch sprigs of berried bayberry with the leaves removed

PUSH a piece of wire midway through the side center of each lemon and lime so that it protrudes an equal distance on each side of the fruit. Bend the wires into a "U" shape toward the stem end of each piece of fruit. ①

Center a lemon at the top of the wreath. Attach the lemon, pointing outward, to the wreath by holding the wire ends 2 inches apart and pushing

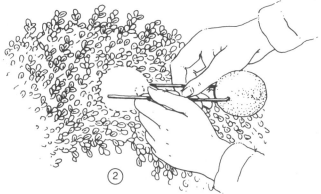

them through the middle of the boxwood.② Twist the wires several times at the back of the wreath to secure the lemon.③ Cut off any excess wire.

Center a lemon at each side and at the bottom of the wreath. Attach them in the same manner. Add a lime above, below, and at each side of the 4 attached lemons, attaching the limes on their sides in the same manner as the lemons.④

To create the diagonal rows of 3 lemons, attach the center lemons, pointing outward, midway between the lemon-lime clusters. Position and attach a lemon on either side of the center lemons in each of the diagonals as shown in the illustration.⑤

Tuck the sprigs of bayberry into the boxwood around the 4 clusters of lemons and limes.⑥

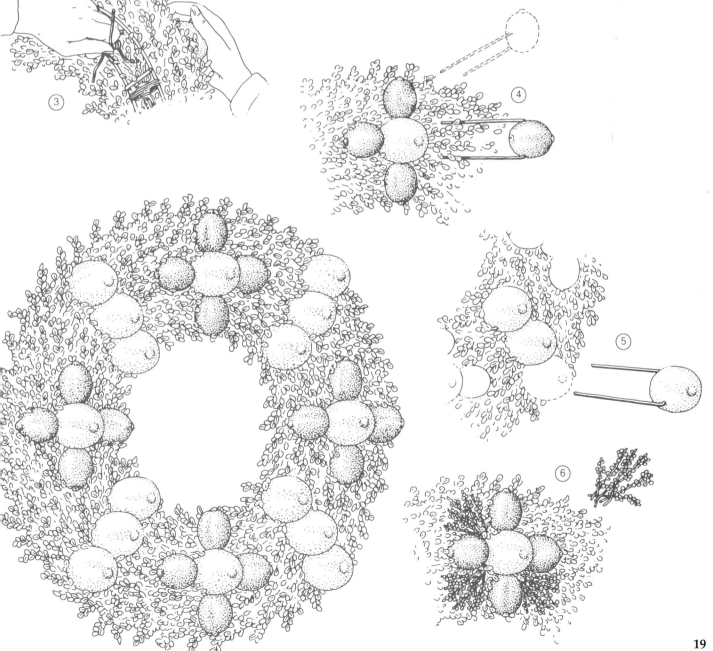

Mixed Fruit Wreath

1 basic boxwood wreath constructed on an 18-inch
  wreath frame (page 10)
32 pieces of #16 gauge floral wire in 18-inch lengths
4 small pomegranates
Wire cutters
12 lady apples that are uniform in size
12 lemons that are uniform in size
4 small oranges
6 4-inch floral picks
6 magnolia pods that are uniform in size
4- to 6-inch sprigs of pyracantha with berries

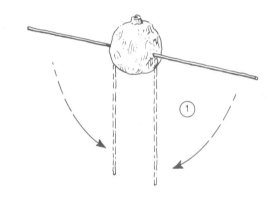

PUSH a piece of wire midway through the side
center of each pomegranate, lady apple, lemon,
and orange so that it protrudes an equal distance
on each side of the fruit. Bend the wires into a
"U" shape toward the stem end of each piece of
fruit. ①

Center a pomegranate at the top of the wreath.
Face the blossom end of the pomegranate outward. Attach the pomegranate to the wreath by
holding the wire ends 2 inches apart and pushing
them through the middle of the boxwood. ②
Twist the wires several times at the back of the
wreath to secure the pomegranate. ③ Cut off any
excess wire. Center a pomegranate at each side
and at the bottom of the wreath. Attach them in
the same manner.

Center a lady apple above and below the top
and bottom pomegranates. Center 2 lady apples,

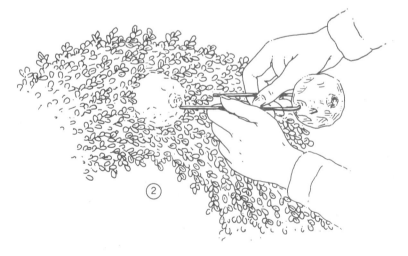

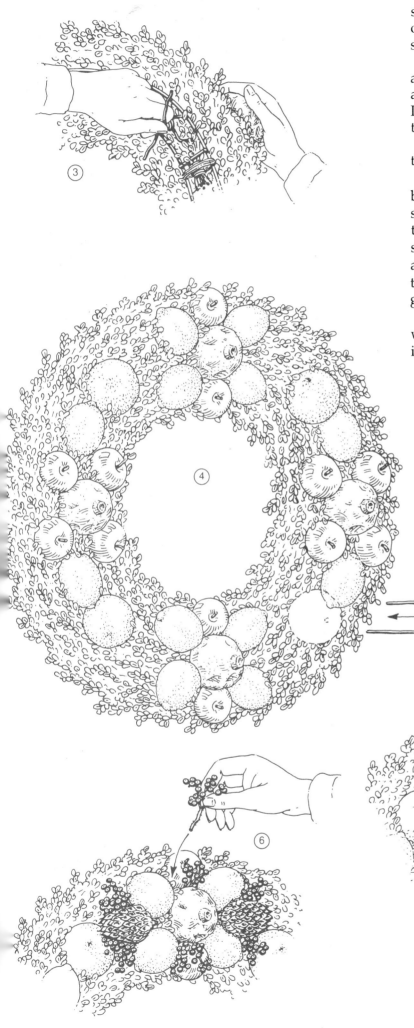

side by side, above and below the pomegranates on each side of the wreath. Attach them in the same manner.

Position and attach 4 lemons on their sides around the pomegranate at the top of the wreath and 4 around the pomegranate at the bottom. Position and attach 1 lemon above and 1 below the lady apples on each side of the wreath.

Position and attach the 4 oranges as shown in the illustration. ④

Wire the magnolia pods on 4-inch floral picks by wrapping the wire on the picks around the stems tightly several times. Bring the wire below the stem and wrap it around the floral pick only several times. Stick 1 magnolia pod to the right and 1 to the left of the top pomegranate and 2 to the right and 2 to the left of the bottom pomegranate. ⑤

Tuck the sprigs of pyracantha into the boxwood at the top and bottom of the wreath as illustrated. ⑥

George Wythe House Matching Wreaths

1 basic boxwood wreath constructed on a 12-inch wreath
frame
6 pieces of #16 gauge floral wire
in 18-inch lengths

6 medium lady apples
Wire cutters
36 4-inch floral picks
12 small scrub pine cones
8 empty cotton bolls

4 medium okra pods
12 bunches of multiflora rose hips
with approximately 3 to 4 stems
in each bunch

PUSH a piece of wire midway through the side center of each lady apple so that it protrudes an equal distance on each side of the apple. Bend the wires into a "U" shape toward the base of each lady apple.①

Center a lady apple at the top of the wreath. Attach the apple to the wreath by holding the wire ends 2 inches apart and pushing them through the middle of the boxwood. Twist the wires several times at the back of the wreath to secure the lady apple.② Cut off any excess wire.

Center an apple at the bottom of the wreath. Position 2 apples, 1 above the other, on each side of the wreath as shown in the illustration.③ Attach them in the same manner.

Wire the scrub pine cones on 4-inch floral picks by looping the wire on the pick in and around the bottom row of scales on the cone. Wrap the wire tightly around the floral pick several times.

Wire the cotton bolls on 4-inch floral picks by wrapping the wire on the pick around the stems tightly several times. Bring the wire below the stem and wrap it around the floral pick several times.

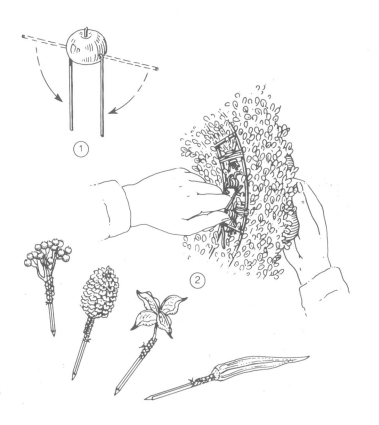

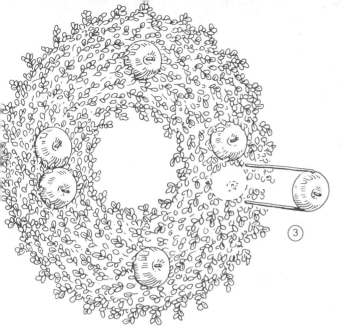

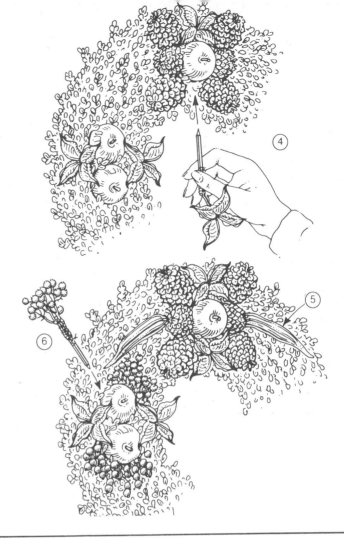

Wire the okra pods and the bunches of rose hips in the same manner.

Insert 3 scrub pine cones on each side of the lady apples at the top and bottom of the wreath.

Insert 1 cotton boll above and below the top and bottom lady apples. Place a cotton boll to the right and left of each pair of lady apples. ④

Insert 1 okra pod on each side of the pine cones at the top and bottom of the wreath. ⑤

Insert 3 bunches of rose hips above and below each pair of lady apples. ⑥

Brush-Everard House Wreath of Lemons, Limes, and Natural Materials

1 basic boxwood wreath constructed on an 18-inch wreath
   frame (page 10)
20 pieces of #16 gauge floral wire
   in 18-inch lengths
8 limes that are uniform in size

12 lemons that are uniform in size
Wire cutters
4 4-inch floral picks
55-66 3-inch floral picks
4 lotus pods
15-18 empty cotton bolls

12 clusters of sweet gum balls with
   approximately 3 sweet gum balls
   in each cluster
18-24 clusters of chinaberries with
   approximately 5 stems in each
   cluster
10-12 small scrub pine cones

PUSH a piece of wire midway through the side center of each lime and lemon so that it protrudes an equal distance on each side of the fruit. Bend the wires into a "U" shape toward the stem end of each piece of fruit. ①

Center a lime at the top of the wreath. Attach the lime, pointing outward, to the wreath by holding the wire ends 2 inches apart and pushing them through the middle of the boxwood. Twist the wires several times at the back of the wreath to secure the lime.② Cut off any excess wire.

Center a lime at each side and at the bottom of the wreath. Attach them in the same manner.

Position and attach a lime on the inside of the wreath next to each of the first 4 limes.

Continued

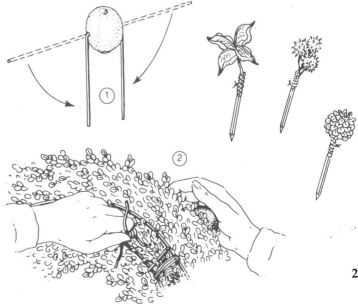

Position and attach 3 lemons around each of the limes as shown in the illustration. ③

Wire the lotus pods on 4-inch floral picks by wrapping the wire on the pick around the stems tightly several times. Bring the wire below the stem and wrap it around the floral pick only several times.

Wire the cotton bolls on 3-inch floral picks in the same manner.

Wire the sweet gum balls on 3-inch floral picks with 3 stems on each pick in the same manner.

Wire the clusters of chinaberries on 3-inch floral picks with approximately 5 stems in each cluster in the same manner.

Wire the scrub pine cones on 3-inch floral picks by looping the wire on the pick in and around the bottom row of scales on the cone. Wrap the wire tightly around the floral pick several times.

Stick the 4 lotus pods into the wreath midway between the lemon-lime clusters.

Stick the cotton bolls, sweet gum balls, and pine cones into the wreath at random.

Fill in spaces by sticking the clusters of chinaberries into the boxwood. The wreath should be very compact. ④

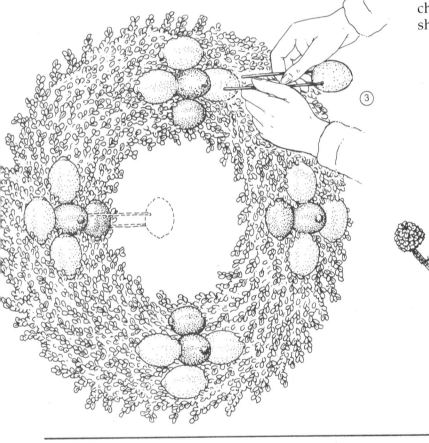

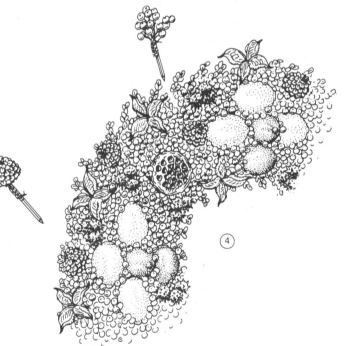

Governor's Palace Pomegranate Wreath

1 basic boxwood wreath constructed on an 18-inch wreath frame (page 10)
3 large pomegranates that have good blossom ends
Sharp knife
3 pieces of #16 gauge floral wire in 18-inch lengths

Wire cutters
9 magnolia leaves
Clippers
4- to 6-inch sprigs of holly berries with the leaves removed

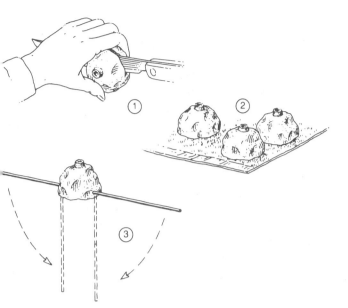

CUT the pomegranates in half horizontally with the knife.① Place the halves on paper towels, cut sides down, until dry (approximately one-half hour).②

Use the 3 blossom end halves. Push a piece of wire through each pomegranate half 1 inch from the cut edge so that it protrudes an equal distance on each side of the pomegranate. Bend the wires into a "U" shape toward the cut side of each pomegranate half.③

Center a pomegranate half at the top of the wreath. Attach the pomegranate half to the wreath by holding the wire ends 3 inches apart and pushing them through the middle of the boxwood.④ Twist the wires several times at the back of the wreath to secure the pomegranate half.⑤ Cut off any excess wire.

Position the other pomegranate halves a little above the middle of each side of the wreath as shown in the illustration. Attach them in the same manner.

Cut off the stems and trim the bases of the magnolia leaves with the clippers. Tuck 3 magnolia leaves under each pomegranate half as shown in the illustration.

Tuck 2 to 3 sprigs of holly berries into the boxwood under each pomegranate half to form a cluster at the base of each magnolia leaf.⑥

25

Traditional Mixed Fruit Wreath

1 basic boxwood wreath constructed on a 20-inch wreath frame
20 pieces of #16 gauge floral wire in 18-inch lengths
2 oranges
6 medium red Delicious apples
6 limes
6 lemons
20-24 small white pine cones
20-24 4-inch floral picks

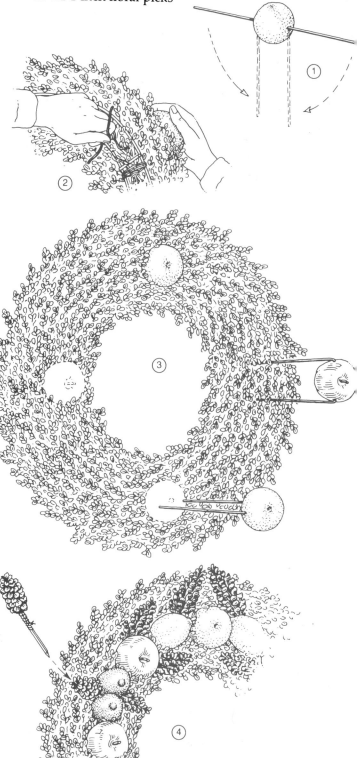

PUSH a piece of wire midway through the side center of each orange, apple, lime, and lemon so that it protrudes an equal distance on each side of the fruit. Bend the wires into a "U" shape toward the stem end of each piece of fruit. ①

Center an orange at the top of the wreath. Attach the orange to the wreath by holding the wire ends· 2 inches apart and pushing them through the middle of the boxwood. Twist the wires several times at the back of the wreath to secure the orange. ② Cut off any excess wire. Center the second orange at the bottom of the wreath. Attach it in the same manner.

Center an apple at each side of the wreath. ③ Attach them in the same manner. Position and attach an apple above and below the center apples as shown in the illustration.

Position and attach a lime on each side of the orange at the bottom of the wreath. Position and attach 2 limes between the top and middle apple on each side of the wreath.

Position and attach a lemon on each side of the orange at the top of the wreath. Position and attach a lemon on each side of the lower apple on each side of the wreath as shown in the illustration.

Wire the white pine cones on 4-inch floral picks by looping the wire on the pick in and around the bottom row of scales on the cone. Wrap the wire tightly around the floral pick several times.

Stick the pine cones into the wreath as shown in the illustration. ④

Pine Cone Flower Wreath

1 basic boxwood wreath constructed on an 8-
   inch wreath frame
Clippers
1 loblolly pine cone
2 scrub pine cones
3 4-inch floral picks
1 yard of ⅝-inch red velvet ribbon
3- to 4-inch sprigs of holly berries with the
   leaves removed

CUT off the top of the loblolly pine cone with the clippers. ①

Wire the loblolly pine cone flower on a 4-inch floral pick by looping the wire on the pick in and around the bottom row of scales on the cone. Wrap the wire tightly around the floral pick several times.

Wire the scrub pine cones in the same manner.

Stick the loblolly pine cone flower into the bottom center of the wreath.

Stick a scrub pine cone to the upper right and upper left of the center cone.

Tuck the sprigs of holly berries into the box-wood above the center cone and at the tips of the scrub pine cones. ②

Loop the red velvet ribbon around the wreath. Bring the 2 ends of the ribbon together. Hang the wreath and adjust the length of the ribbon. ③

Trim the ends of the ribbon if they show.

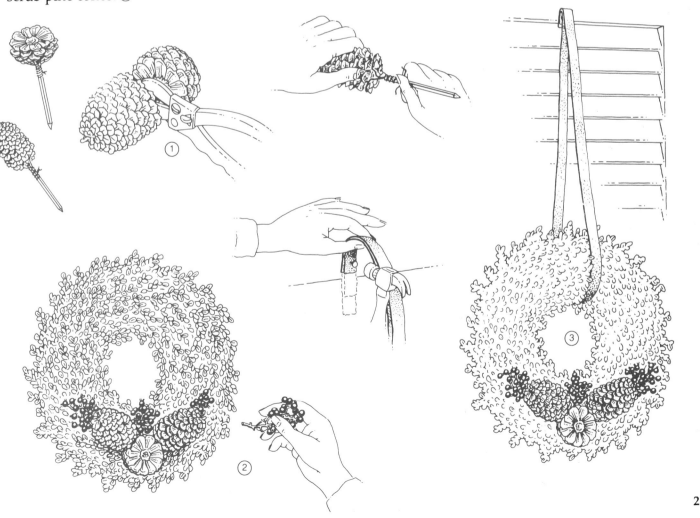

27

Plaque of Lady Apples and Pine Cones

1 green styrofoam sheet 8 inches
   long x 6 inches wide x 2 inches
   thick
24-29 large magnolia leaves
Clippers
36-43 floral pins

61-77 4-inch floral picks
6-8 8-inch twigs of scrub pine
12-14 lady apples
15-20 scrub pine cones
10-15 small magnolia leaves

10-12 4- to 6-inch twigs of scrub
   pine
6- to 8-inch sprigs of boxwood
15-20 6-inch sprigs of berried
   bayberry with the leaves removed

USE a sheet of styrofoam 8 inches long x 6 inches wide x 2 inches thick for a standard door. ① The finished decoration will be larger than the styrofoam base.

Cut the stem ends off of 12-14 large magnolia leaves with the clippers. Cover the 4 sides of the styrofoam by wrapping the magnolia leaves around the sides. Secure the leaves with floral pins. ② Use enough leaves to hide the styrofoam.

Wire the 8-inch scrub pine twigs on 4-inch floral picks by wrapping the wire on the pick around the stems tightly several times. Bring the wire below the stem and wrap it around the floral pick only several times. Stick the twigs into the top and bottom of the styrofoam. ③ Curved twigs give a more graceful look.

Cut the stem ends off of 12-15 large magnolia leaves with the clippers. Attach the magnolia leaves to the styrofoam with floral pins so that they radiate from the center. ④ The tips of the leaves should point outward.

Impale the lady apples on 4-inch floral picks. Insert them in the center of the design. Build up the design with the lady apples. ⑤ Be sure that the lady apples are secure and that the picks are inserted well into the styrofoam.

Wire the scrub pine cones on 4-inch floral picks by looping the wire on the pick in and around the bottom row of scales on the cone. Wrap the wire tightly around the floral pick several times. Insert the scrub pine cones around and between the lady apples. ⑥

Wire the 4- to 6-inch scrub pine twigs on 4-inch floral picks. ⑦ Fill in spaces, especially along the sides of the design, with the 4- to 6-inch scrub pine twigs.

Wire 10-15 small magnolia leaves on 4-inch floral picks as shown in the illustration. ⑧ Tuck in the magnolia leaves. The magnolia leaves and scrub pine twigs will give the design depth.

Tuck in a few sprigs of boxwood. ⑨

Tuck the sprigs of bayberry in among the lady apples and pine cones. ⑩

NOTE: This is a good decoration to make in duplicate for divided doors.

Plaque Featuring Fruit and Natural Materials

1 green styrofoam sheet 10 inches
  long x 5 inches wide x 2 inches
  thick
12-14 large magnolia leaves
Clippers
62-66 floral pins
27-30 6-inch floral picks
30-32 4-inch floral picks
6 10- to 12-inch twigs of white
  pine
28-30 6-inch twigs of scrub pine

18 pieces of #18 gauge floral wire
  in 18-inch lengths
8 okra pods
8 honey locust pods
2 large lotus pods
1 dried sunflower 5 inches in
  diameter with a 6-inch stem
4 dried artichokes
4 6-inch hyacinth stakes
7 lemons
2 medium oranges
9 9-inch hyacinth stakes

5-6 milkweed pods
4 clusters of sweet gum balls with
  3 stems in each cluster
Brown floral tape
8 clusters of chinaberries with approximately 5 stems in each
  cluster
8 yarrow flowers with 6- to 8-inch
  stems
2 white pine cones
4-6 empty cotton bolls

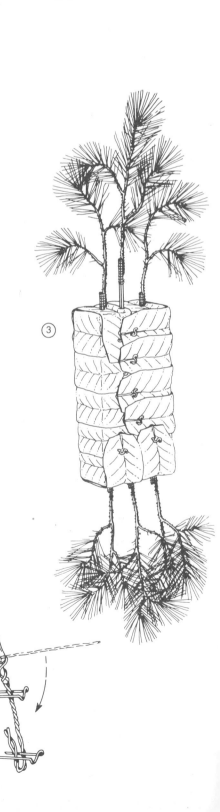

USE a sheet of styrofoam 10 inches long x 5 inches wide x 2 inches thick for a standard door.① The finished decoration will be larger than the styrofoam base.

Cut the stem ends off of 12-14 magnolia leaves with the clippers. Cover the 4 sides of the styrofoam by wrapping the magnolia leaves around the sides. Secure the leaves with floral pins.② Use enough leaves to hide the styrofoam.

Wire the 10- to 12-inch white pine twigs on 6-inch floral picks by wrapping the wire on the pick around the stems tightly several times. Bring the wire below the stem and wrap it around the floral pick only several times. Wire the 6-inch scrub pine twigs on 4-inch floral picks in the same manner. Stick 3 white pine twigs into the top and 3 into the bottom of the styrofoam.③ Curved twigs give a more graceful look. Stick 20 of the 6-inch scrub pine twigs in between the longer twigs at the top and bottom and also along the sides of the styrofoam.④

Wire the okra pods as shown in the illustration. Leave twisted 6- to 9-inch wire tails.

Wire the locust pods and lotus pods in the same manner.

Center an okra pod at the top of the plaque. Form a loop with the wire tail. Secure the okra pod with floral pins as shown in the illustration. Position and attach the other okra pods as shown in the illustration.⑤

Place the honey locust pods between the okra pods and attach them in the same manner.⑥

Place the lotus pods at the top left and bottom center of the design. Attach them in the same manner.⑦

Position the dried sunflower at the top center of the plaque and attach the stem securely with floral pins.⑧

Impale the dried artichokes on 6-inch hyacinth stakes. Insert an artichoke at the top, bottom, and each side of the styrofoam base.⑨

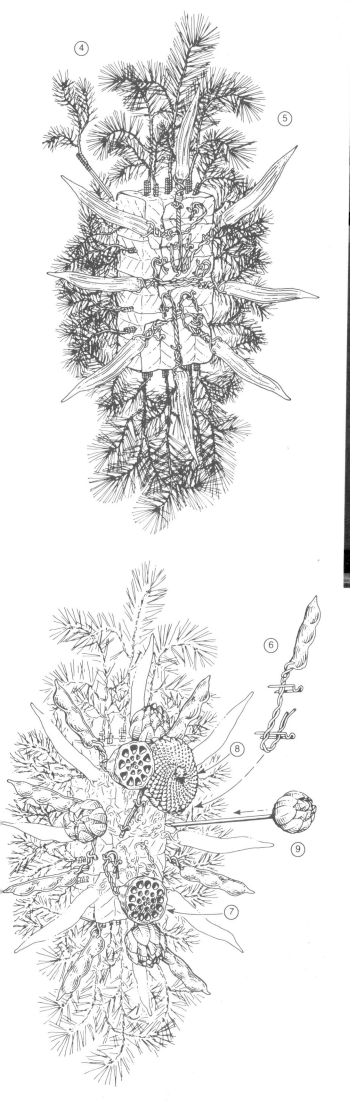

Impale the lemons and oranges on 9-inch hyacinth stakes. Insert the lemons at random as shown in the illustration.⑩ Insert the oranges more toward the center of the design. ⑪

Split open and empty the milkweed pods. Wire the milkweed pods on 6-inch floral picks. Place them throughout the design. ⑫

Wire the sweet gum balls on 6-inch floral picks with 3 stems on each pick. Wrap the picks with brown floral tape. Insert the sweet gum balls at the top, sides, and bottom of the design. ⑬

Wire the clusters of chinaberries on 6-inch floral picks with approximately 5 stems in each cluster. ⑭

Fill in spaces with the clusters of chinaberries and the yarrow.⑮

Wire the white pine cones on 4-inch floral picks by looping the wire on the pick in and around the bottom row of scales on the cone. Wrap the wire tightly around the floral pick several times. ⑯

Wire the cotton bolls on 6-inch floral picks.⑰

Continued

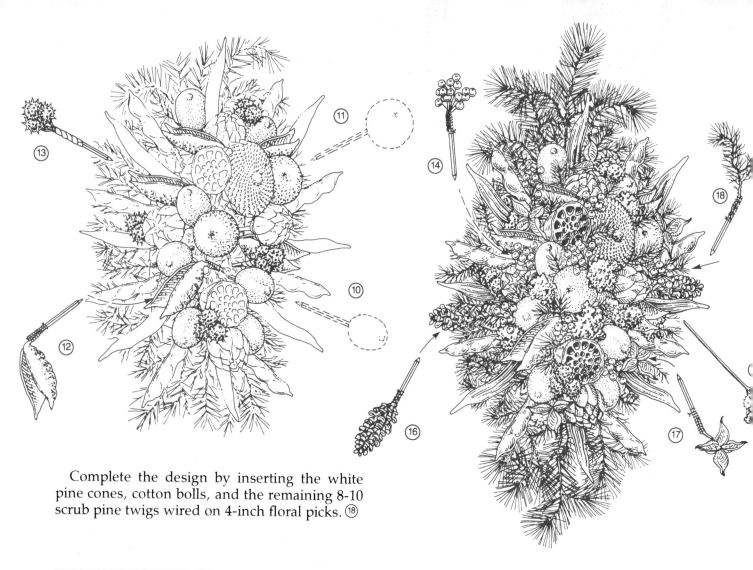

Complete the design by inserting the white pine cones, cotton bolls, and the remaining 8-10 scrub pine twigs wired on 4-inch floral picks. ⑱

James Geddy House Red Peppers Plaque

1 green styrofoam sheet
   8 inches long x 6 inches wide
   x 2 inches thick
24-29 large magnolia leaves
Clippers
36-43 floral pins
6 8-inch twigs of scrub pine

34-39 4-inch floral picks
10 pieces of #18 gauge floral
   wire in 18-inch lengths
8 okra pods
2 large lotus pods
10-12 lady apples
15 scrub pine cones
47-61 6-inch floral picks

8-10 4-inch twigs of scrub
   pine
50 hot red peppers
Green floral tape
10 empty cotton bolls
10-15 sweet gum balls
10-15 small magnolia leaves

USE a sheet of styrofoam 8 inches long x 6 inches wide x 2 inches thick for a standard door. ① The finished decoration will be larger than the styrofoam base.

Cut the stem ends off of 12-14 large magnolia leaves with the clippers. Cover the 4 sides of the styrofoam by wrapping the magnolia leaves around the sides. Secure the leaves with floral pins. ② Use enough leaves to hide the styrofoam.

Wire the 8-inch scrub pine twigs on 4-inch floral picks by wrapping the wire on the pick

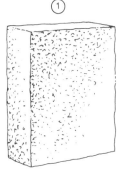

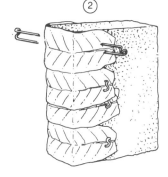

around the stems tightly several times. Bring the wire below the stem and wrap it around the floral pick only several times. Stick 3 twigs into the top and 3 into the bottom of the styrofoam. Curved twigs give a more graceful look. ③

Cut the stem ends off of 12-15 large magnolia leaves with the clippers. Attach the magnolia leaves to the styrofoam with floral pins so that they radiate from the center. ④ The tips of the leaves should point outward.

Wire the okra pods as shown in the illustration. Leave twisted 6- to 9-inch tails.

Wire the lotus pods in the same manner.

Center an okra pod at the top of the plaque. Form a loop with the wire tail. Secure the okra pod with floral pins as shown in the illustration. Position and attach the other okra pods as shown in the illustration. ⑤

Place the lotus pods in the center of the plaque and attach them in the same manner. ⑥

Impale the lady apples on 4-inch floral picks. Insert the lady apples around and between the lotus pods as shown in the illustration. ⑦

Wire 5 scrub pine cones on 4-inch floral picks by looping the wire on the pick in and around the bottom row of scales on the cone. ⑧ Wrap the wire tightly around the floral pick several times. Wire 10 scrub pine cones on 6-inch floral picks in the same manner. Insert the scrub pine cones on 4-inch floral picks around and between the lady apples.

Place the scrub pine cones wired on 6-inch floral picks around the outside edge of the design.

Wire the 4-inch scrub pine twigs on 4-inch floral picks. Insert a few of the scrub pine twigs between the lady apples. ⑨

Wire 35 hot red peppers on 6-inch floral picks with 2-3 peppers on each pick. Wire 15 hot red peppers on 4-inch floral picks with 2-3 peppers

Continued

on each pick. Wrap the brittle red pepper stems with green floral tape. Insert the peppers on the 6-inch floral picks at the top and bottom of the design and the peppers on 4-inch picks around the lotus pods. ⑩

Fill in spaces with the remaining 4-inch scrub pine twigs. ⑪

Wire the cotton bolls on 6-inch floral picks. ⑫

Wire the sweet gum balls on 6-inch floral picks with 2-3 stems on each pick. Wrap the picks with green floral tape. ⑬ Insert the cotton bolls and sweet gum balls.

Wire the small magnolia leaves on 6-inch floral picks as shown in the illustration. ⑭ Tuck them in to give the design depth.

Apple Fan

1 piece of ½ inch thick plywood board cut into a fan shape to fit the top of the door frame. The board illustrated is 40 inches long x 12 inches high in the center.
Hammer
30 eightpenny finishing nails
3 tenpenny finishing nails
1 fourpenny box nail
1 piece of #22 gauge floral wire 12 inches in length

3 screw hooks
3 screw eyes
Staple gun with staples
22 large magnolia leaves that are uniform in size
Clippers
80 3-inch sprigs of boxwood
30 large red Delicious apples
1 medium to large pineapple
3 pieces of #16 gauge floral wire in 6-inch lengths

BEGIN at the lower right corner of the frame 2½ inches from the outer edge. Drive a row of 7 eightpenny finishing nails into the board approximately 3 inches apart along the outer curve and ending just to the right of center.① The row of nails should slant upward 1¾ inches from the board. The center space will be filled by the pineapple.

Leave 4 inches between the rows of nails. Drive in another row of 5 upward slanting nails 3 inches apart.② Drive in the last row of 3 upward slanting nails 3 inches apart.③

leaves protrude outward 3 to 4 inches from the edge of the board.⑧

Staple 3-inch sprigs of boxwood onto the board so that it is covered.⑨ Some sprigs of boxwood should cover the stem ends of the magnolia leaves.⑩ Staple sprigs of boxwood along the edges of the board.

Impale an apple on each nail. The stem end should face outward. ⑪

Continued

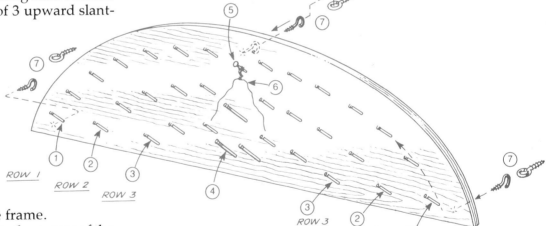

ROW 1 ROW 2 ROW 3

ROW 3 ROW 2 ROW 1

Repeat on the left side of the frame.

Drive the 3 tenpenny nails into the center of the frame in a triangle.④ Drive the fourpenny nail into the frame above the triangle 3½ inches from the top center edge.⑤ Twist the piece of #22 gauge floral wire around the nail.⑥ It will be used to secure the pineapple top.

Attach a screw hook on the back of the board at the center top 2 inches from the edge. Attach a screw hook at each corner 2 inches in from the edges.⑦ Attach corresponding screw eyes on the building.

Cut the stem ends off of 22 magnolia leaves with the clippers. Staple 20 magnolia leaves to the top curve of the board in a fan shape so that the

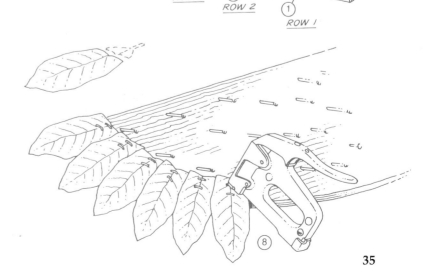

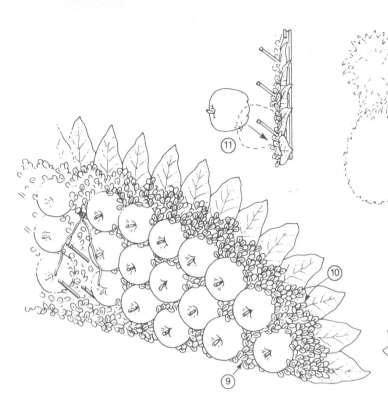

Impale the pineapple on the 3 nails in the center of the board. Wrap the wire through the leaves of the pineapple to secure it. Twist the wire several times in back of the pineapple foliage.⑫

Staple 2 magnolia leaves at the base of the pineapple as illustrated. The stem ends should be tucked under the pineapple.⑬

To secure the board to the building, hook the screw hooks through the screw eyes. Wrap a piece of #16 gauge floral wire around each hook and eye.⑭

Decoration for a Windowsill

2 18-inch balsam branches
3 pieces of #16 gauge floral wire
 in 18-inch lengths
2 pieces of chenille wire in 18-
 inch lengths
1 piece of styrofoam 4 inches
 wide x 10 inches long x 2
 inches thick

Hammer
2 nails
20-30 8- to 10-inch balsam twigs
8 medium red Delicious apples
13 large lemons

21 4-inch floral picks
8 medium white pine cones
8 8-inch floral picks
6 small white pine cones
6 6-inch floral picks

THIS decoration will measure approximately 30 inches across.

The back of the decoration is prepared first. Wire the balsam branches together tightly with 1 piece of floral wire, overlapping the branches 6 inches.① Push 1 piece of chenille wire through the styrofoam 2 inches from 1 end as shown in the illustration. Repeat with the other piece of chenille wire.② Lay the balsam branches on the styrofoam.③ Bring the 2 chenille wires around the branches and twist the wires together.④

Wrap 2 pieces of floral wire around the balsam branches at the back of the decoration as shown in the illustration. Twist the wires together leaving 8-inch ends.⑤

The decoration is now ready to be attached to the windowsill.

Hammer 2 nails inside the windowsill 2 inches

from the left and right of the center of the sill.⑥ Wrap the wires on the back of the decoration around the nails in the sill as shown in the illustration.⑦ All wiring must be secure since the decoration will become heavy as fruit and plant materials are added. Close the window.

Stick the balsam twigs into the styrofoam so that the front is covered. ⑧

Continued

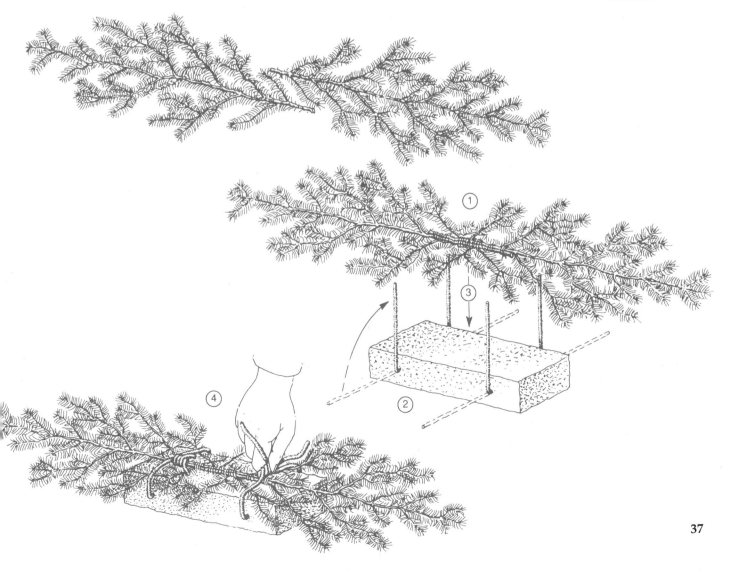

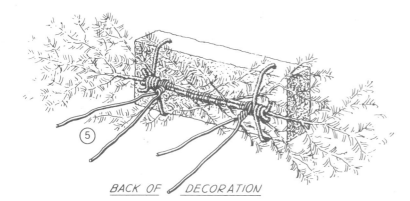

BACK OF DECORATION

Impale the apples and lemons on 4-inch floral picks.⑨ Arrange the fruit as shown in the illustration.⑩

Wire the medium white pine cones on 8-inch floral picks by looping the wire on the pick in and around the bottom row of scales on the cone.⑪ Wire the small white pine cones on 6-inch floral picks in the same manner. Arrange the cones so that they radiate outward from the center.⑫

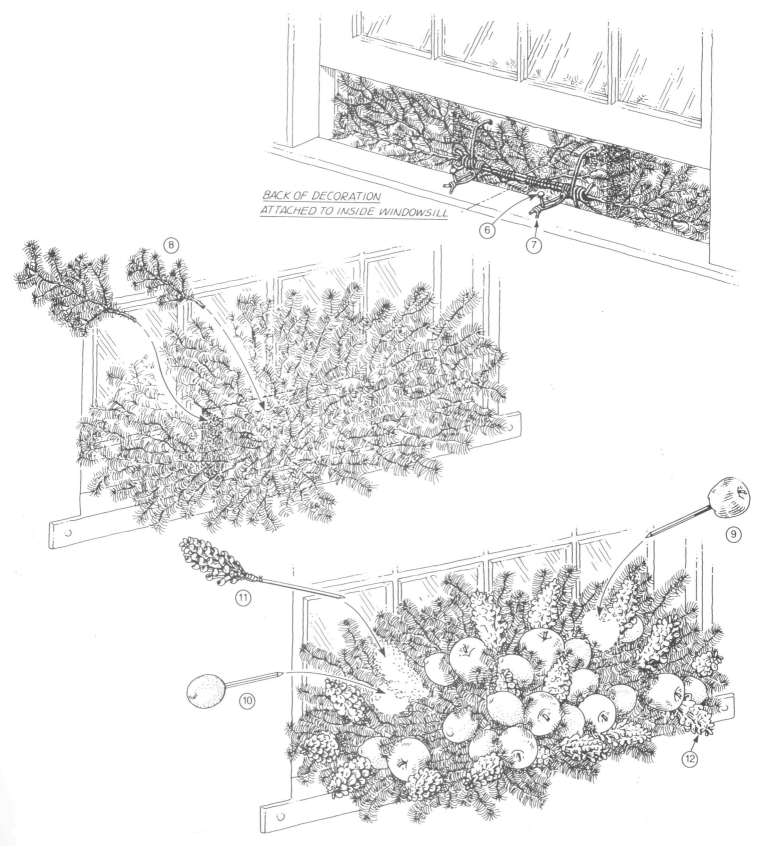

BACK OF DECORATION
ATTACHED TO INSIDE WINDOWSILL

Table
Decorations

Mixed Fruit Curve with Nuts and Berries

1 circle of heavy green plastic 30 inches in diameter, cut in half

1 green styrofoam wreath, 26 inches in diameter, cut in half

2 floral pins

40 large magnolia leaves

Clippers

60 4-inch floral picks

77 3-inch floral picks

20 bunches of camellia leaves with 2-inch stems

10 bunches of English holly with 2-inch stems

20 small oranges

10 medium pomegranates

10 lady apples

20 small lemons

12 limes

4 bunches of red grapes

4 clusters of English walnuts

3 clusters of hickory nuts

6 clusters of acorns

4 clusters of buckeyes

4 clusters of peach pits

CUT the plastic 4 inches wider than the styrofoam and in the same shape. Center the plastic on the table in an "S" shape. Place the 2 sections of the styrofoam wreath on top of the "S"-shaped plastic. Anchor the 2 pieces of styrofoam at the middle with the floral pins. ①

Cut off the stems and trim the bases of the magnolia leaves with the clippers.

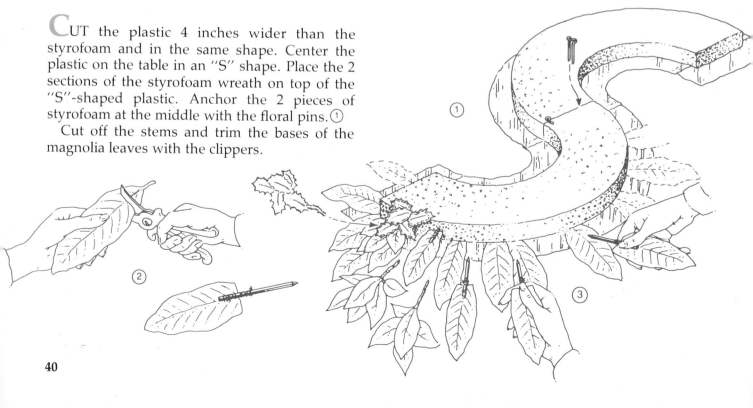

Lay some of the largest magnolia leaves partially under the styrofoam so that they conceal the plastic and form a background for the decoration. Wire half of the remaining magnolia leaves on 4-inch floral picks and the other half on 3-inch floral picks.② Clip the stems of the bunches of camellia leaves and English holly at an angle so that it will be easier to insert them into the styrofoam.

Stick the greens into the sides of the styrofoam, beginning at the base of the decoration and making it wider at the base.③ Intersperse the individual magnolia leaves equally with the bunches of camellia leaves and the English holly. Some of the greens should be inserted at an angle.④ Leave the top of the styrofoam bare for placing the fruit.

Impale half of the fruit on 4-inch floral picks and the other half on 3-inch floral picks. Stick the oranges and pomegranates into the styrofoam on the top of the decoration at various angles.⑤ Insert the lady apples, lemons, and limes so that the colors and shapes are seen throughout the design. The smaller fruits may be placed on top of each other or may rest on the larger fruits to create a mounded appearance.

Wire the bunches of red grapes on 4-inch floral picks. Insert them at intervals, draping the clusters among the leaves and fruit. ⑥

The nuts may be attached in one of two ways:

1. Make a hole at the base end of the nut where it was attached to the twig with a sharp instrument or separate the shell slightly. Insert a green pipe cleaner and add glue to be sure that it sticks. Let the nuts dry overnight. To form a cluster, gather several nuts on pipe cleaners together and wind another pipe cleaner around the base of the cluster. Clip off all of the extra lengths of pipe cleaners. Wind the wire on a 4-inch floral pick around the remaining short piece of pipe cleaner and insert the pick into the styrofoam.

2. Place a nut in a vise, gently tightening the vise so that the pressure will not crack the nut. Carefully drill a hole through one end or side of the nut, drilling gradually so that the nut will not shatter. Use a $^3/_{32}$-inch bit for walnuts and peach pits; a $^5/_{64}$-inch bit is better for the smaller nuts. Push a thin wire through the hole in the nut and twist the wire to secure it. Gather several wired nuts into a cluster, then wire them on a 4-inch floral pick. Insert the pick into the styrofoam.

Apple Cone

1 cone-shaped wooden form 10 inches high, 5 inches wide at the base, and 2½ inches wide at the top.

58 2-inch finishing nails have been driven into the form in 9 vertical rows with 6 nails in each row and 4 nails in the top. All of the nails extend outward 1 inch from the base.

The cone is available from Colonial Williamsburg, 201 Fifth Avenue, P.O. Box CH, Williamsburg, Virginia 23187.

15 flat magnolia leaves that are uniform in size
Clippers
Flat plate or cardboard 10 inches in diameter
22-36 medium red Delicious apples
1 large apple for the top or 1 small pineapple
4-inch sprigs of boxwood

THE apple cone is one of the most popular Williamsburg table decorations. It may be done in a variety of ways, 4 of which are illustrated. All of the designs are suitable for a cone to be placed against a wall so that the back does not show. Designs II, III, and IV are also suitable for a cone that is used as a centerpiece and therefore will be viewed from all sides. It is more difficult to create a symmetrical Design I, which has 3 vertical rows of 8 apples each, in the round. The size and shape of the apples available will determine the exact number needed. In general, the largest, fattest apples should be used on the bottom row of the cone and the thinnest apples for the most compact rows. Tucking in sprigs of boxwood to fill spaces between the fruit will greatly improve the appearance of an apple cone.

Cut off the stems and trim the bases of the magnolia leaves with the clippers.① Arrange the leaves so that they cover the plate or cardboard.② The pointed ends should extend beyond the outer edge.

Place the wooden form on top of the leaves.③

Design I: Use the smaller apples for this arrangement, which has 8 apples in each of 3 rows and 1 apple on top. Starting at the bottom of the cone, impale a horizontal row of 8 of the largest apples, evenly spaced. There are 9 nails in the horizontal row so some of the apples must be impaled off center. Impale a second horizontal row of 8 apples directly above the first row. Impale a third horizontal row of the 8 thinnest apples directly above the first two rows. It may be necessary to rearrange the apples in the third row until they fit on the cone. Impale 1 large apple on the top nail. If the apples selected for this arrangement are quite small, 9 may be used in the first 2 rows and 1 or 2 fewer in the third row, arranged in a pleasing way. ④

Design II: This arrangement is created in the same manner as Design I. It features 3 horizontal rows with 7 apples in each row and 1 large apple

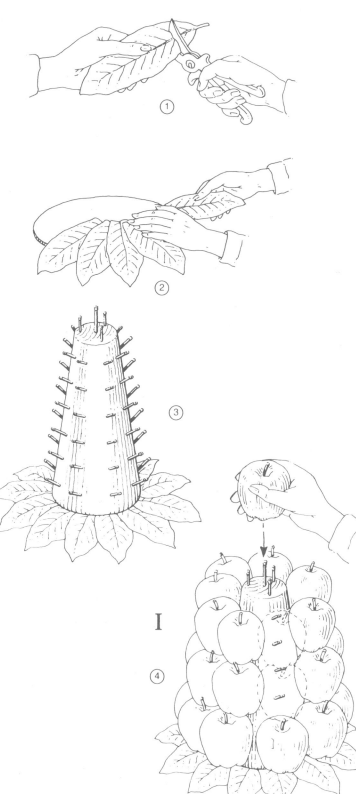

on top. The spaces between the apples will be wider, but they will be filled in with boxwood. ⑤

Design III: Starting at the bottom of the cone, impale a horizontal row of 8 of the largest apples, evenly spaced. Alternate a second horizontal row of 8 apples above the first row. Arrange a third horizontal row of 7 apples in a pleasing way to compensate for the decreasing size of the cone. Impale 1 large apple on the top nail. ⑥

Design IV: Starting at the bottom of the cone, impale a horizontal row of 9 of the largest apples, stems facing outward, with 1 apple on each nail. Alternate a second horizontal row of 9 apples above the first row. The apples in the second row must be impaled off center. Alternate a third horizontal row of 9 of the thinnest apples above the second row. Arrange the fourth row of 8 apples to create a symmetrically pleasing design. Impale 1 large apple, a small pineapple, the top half of a large pineapple, or even pineapple foliage alone on the top nail. ⑦

Tuck in sprigs of boxwood to fill spaces between the apples. ⑧

NOTE: If magnolia leaves are not available, rhododendron or other large, flat leaves may be substituted. Sprigs of holly, white pine, or other bushy foliage may be used in place of the boxwood.

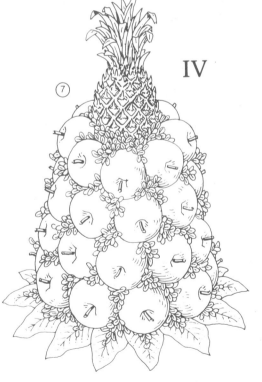

Mixed Fruit Cone

1 cone-shaped wooden form 12 inches high, 5 inches wide at the base, and 2 ½ inches wide at the top. 67 2-inch finishing nails have been driven into the form in 9 vertical rows with 7 nails in each row and 4 nails in the top. All of the nails extend outward 1 inch from the base.

The cone is available from Colonial Williamsburg, 201 Fifth Avenue, P. O. Box CH, Williamsburg, Virginia 23187

12 large flat magnolia leaves that are uniform in size
Clippers

Flat plate or cardboard 10 inches in diameter
7-8 medium red Delicious apples
4-5 small oranges
5-6 lemons
8-9 limes
8-10 lady apples
2 pounds green grapes
30 kumquats
1 small pineapple
3- to 4-inch sprigs of boxwood
6-inch sprigs of boxwood

CUT off the stems and trim the bases of the magnolia leaves with the clippers.① Arrange the leaves so that they cover the plate or cardboard. The pointed ends should extend beyond the outer edge.②

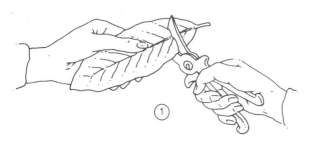

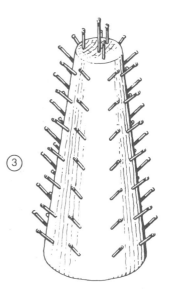

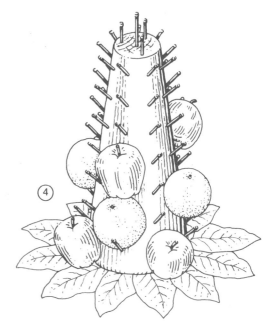

Place the wooden form on top of the leaves.③

Begin with the apples and oranges. Impale them at intervals on the nails. Place more of the apples and oranges toward the base of the cone for balance.④ Add the lemons, limes, and lady apples. Leave spaces between the fruit.⑤ Hang small clusters of green grapes on the nails to fill some of the spaces. Fill the rest of the spaces with the kumquats. ⑥

Impale the pineapple on the top of the cone.⑦

Tuck in sprigs of boxwood to fill spaces between the fruit. Use the longer sprigs of boxwood at the bottom to fill in spaces between the magnolia leaves and the bottom row of fruit.

NOTE: If magnolia leaves are not available, rhododendron or other large, flat leaves may be substituted. Sprigs of holly, white pine, or other bushy foliage may be used in place of the boxwood.

⑤

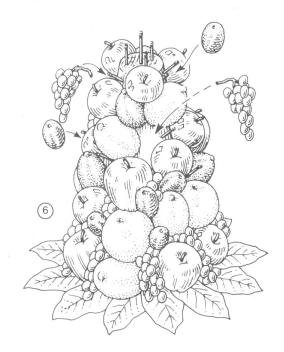

⑥

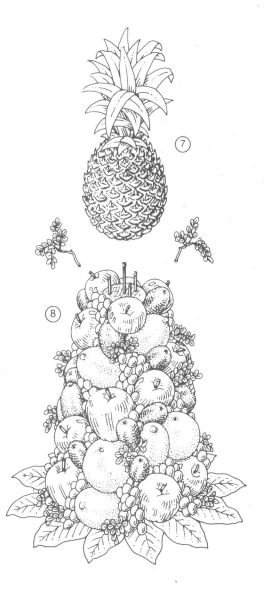

⑦

⑧

Osage Orange Cone

1 cone-shaped wooden form 10 inches high (see
   Apple Cone)
15 flat magnolia leaves that are uniform in size
Clippers
Flat plate or cardboard 10 inches in diameter
20-22 small osage oranges (which are also called
   hedge apples or bois d'arcs)
3- to 4-inch sprigs of variegated English holly
3- to 4-inch sprigs of boxwood
6-inch sprigs of boxwood

CUT off the stems and trim the bases of the
magnolia leaves with the clippers.① Arrange the
leaves so that they cover the plate or cardboard.
The pointed ends should extend beyond the
outer edge.②

Place the wooden form on top of the leaves.③

Begin at the bottom of the form. Impale a
horizontal row of osage oranges on the nails.
Make the bottom row secure by fitting the osage
oranges against each other tightly. Arrange 3
more rows of osage oranges. ④

Impale a well-shaped osage orange on the top
of the form.⑤

Tuck in sprigs of variegated English holly and

boxwood to fill spaces between the fruit.⑥ Use
the longer sprigs of boxwood at the bottom to fill
in spaces between the magnolia leaves and the
bottom row of osage oranges.

NOTE: If magnolia leaves are not available,
rhododendron or other large, flat leaves may be
substituted.

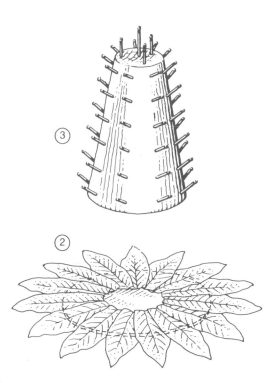

Lemon Cone

1 cone-shaped wooden form 10 inches high
9 flat magnolia leaves that are uniform in size
9 aucuba leaves that are uniform in size
Clippers
Flat plate or cardboard 10 inches in diameter
34 large lemons
4-inch sprigs of boxwood

CUT off the stems and trim the bases of the magnolia and aucuba leaves with the clippers.① Alternate the leaves so that they cover the plate or cardboard. The pointed ends should extend beyond the outer edge. ②

Place the wooden form on top of the leaves. ③

Starting with the bottom row of nails, impale a horizontal row of 9 lemons, spaced equally to compensate for the upward taper of the cone. Use the largest, fattest lemons. The pointed ends of the lemons should point upward. Impale a second row of 9 lemons directly above and touching the first row. Use slightly smaller lemons. Impale a third row of 9 lemons directly above and touching the second row. Use the thinnest lemons and press them in tightly. Impale a fourth row of 6 lemons to create a pleasing arrangement.④

Impale 1 large, perfect lemon on the center top nail.

Tuck in sprigs of boxwood to fill spaces between the lemons. ⑤

NOTE: If magnolia or aucuba leaves are not available, rhododendron or other large, flat leaves may be substituted. Sprigs of holly, white pine, or other bushy foliage may be used in place of the boxwood.

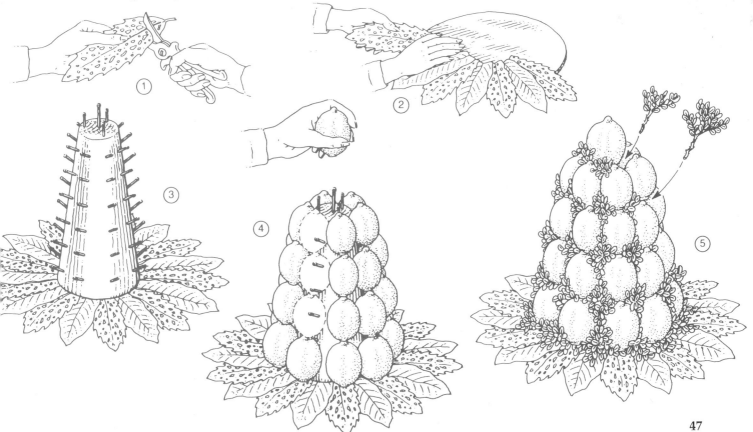

47

Brush-Everard House Table Decoration

1 glass salver 11½ inches in
    diameter and 6 5/16 inches high
1 glass salver 9½ inches in
    diameter and 5⅞ inches high
1 orange cup 3¾ inches in
    diameter and 7 inches high
6 jelly glasses filled with mint jelly
6 birds
4 dishes 3 inches in diameter
2 dishes 7¾ inches in diameter
1 sauceboat
¼ pound candied orange peel

24 marzipan strawberries
4 strips of heavy plastic 2 inches
    wide x 10 inches long
21 limes
2- to 3-inch sprigs of boxwood
2-inch sprigs of white pine with
    the needles uniformly
    trimmed

2- to 3-inch sprigs of holly berries
    with a few leaves left on
18-20 small lady apples
¼ pound green grapes

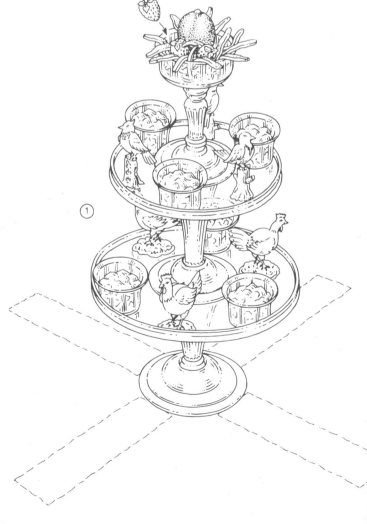

PLACE the 2 salvers in the center of the table with the smaller salver on top of the larger. Place the orange cup on top of the smaller salver. Place 3 filled jelly glasses on each salver. Place 3 birds on each salver. Add sprigs of white pine and holly to the bottom salver.

Fill the orange cup with candied orange peel and nestle a lime in the center. Surround the lime with 4 marzipan strawberries.

Place the 4 strips of plastic so that they radiate from the base of the salvers toward the edges of the table. ①

Place 1 small dish at the end of each strip of plastic. Arrange the 2 larger dishes and the sauceboat in the design.

Arrange the limes in matching designs on the plastic strips. ②

Use sprigs of boxwood to conceal the plastic. Add trimmed sprigs of white pine around the limes to add texture. Tuck in the holly sprigs last. ③

48

Arrange candied orange peel and marzipan strawberries in the 4 small dishes.

Fill the 2 large dishes with lady apples and loose green grapes. ④

The antique porcelain birds and the sauceboat are an integral part of this design. We suggest that you substitute objects d'art of your own.

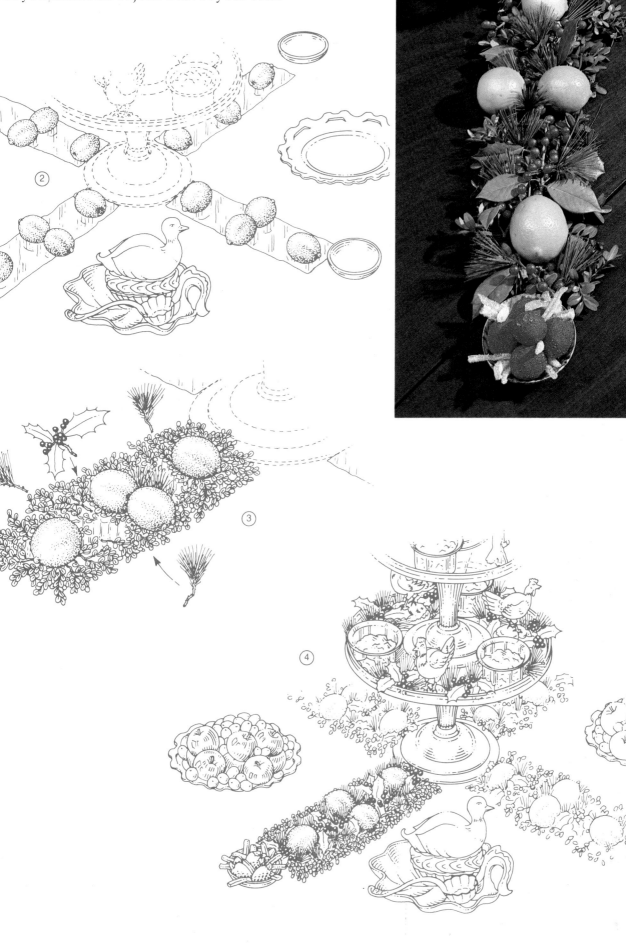

Epergne

1 silver epergne 12 ¾ inches high, 19 ⅜ inches long,
  and 18 ⅛ inches wide. The center basket is 4 5/16
  inches wide, 14 ¼ inches long, and 9 ⅜ inches
  wide. The 4 saucers are 5 ¾ inches in diameter.
Plastic cut to fit the center and the 4 saucers of the
  epergne
11 small lemons

4 pears
4 medium red Delicious apples
3 limes
5 pounds of red grapes. Be sure to include 2 attractive clusters for draping.
1 small pineapple
8 lady apples

LINE the bottom of the center of the epergne with the plastic to protect it from the fruit. Center the epergne on the table.

Arrange 5 lemons side by side lengthwise across the bottom.① Arrange 3 lemons on top of them side by side widthwise, using the smallest lemon in the center.② To complete the side shown in the illustration, place 1 pear in each hollow area formed by the base of the lemons.③ Center a lemon between the 2 pears. On the other side, place an apple in each of the 2 hollow areas. Center a lime between the 2 apples.④ Place a cluster of grapes at each end of the container.⑤ Be sure that the heavier ends of the clusters are securely placed in the container. The clusters should droop evenly. Place a small pineapple in the center of the container.⑥ Work small clusters of grapes and lady apples in and around the pineapple.⑦

Line the 4 saucers with plastic. Opposite saucers should be arranged identically.

Place an apple, a lime, and a few small clusters of grapes on 2 of the saucers. Complete the arrangement by adding a lady apple.⑧

Place a pear, a lemon, and a lady apple on the other 2 saucers. Complete the arrangement by adding a few small clusters of grapes.⑨

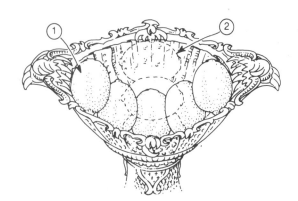

NOTE: The amount of fruit needed to create this decoration may be adjusted depending on the size of the container used. The kind and size of fruit available will vary with the season; it is important, however, to maintain a sense of proportion by using a variety of shapes and colors. Wooden toothpicks may be used to impale small fruits onto the pineapple, but punctured fruit will deteriorate rapidly. If a small pineapple is not available, the top of a larger one may be used.

Table Decoration Featuring Oranges and Limes

2 strips of orange ribbon 48 inches long x
    3 inches wide
1 10-inch bone china bowl in the "Chinese
    Tiger" pattern
Plastic cut to fit the inside of the bowl
20 medium oranges
20 limes
4 spruce cones
Clippers
3- to 3 ½-inch sprigs of boxwood

CRISS cross the ribbons on the table, centering them.

Line the bottom of the bowl with the plastic to protect it from the fruit. Center the bowl on the table where the ribbons overlap. ① Arrange 12 oranges and 12 limes in the bowl. ②

Cut each spruce cone into 3 sections with the clippers. ③

Begin next to the bowl. Arrange a sprig of boxwood next to the bowl on each section of ribbon. Center an orange on each sprig of boxwood. Placing fruit on the boxwood will hold it stationary. Leave a space for the ribbon to show

through. Place a cut section of cone on each ribbon. Arrange a second sprig of boxwood on each ribbon. Center a lime on each sprig of boxwood, then add another cut section of cone. Arrange another sprig of boxwood on each ribbon and add a second orange. Arrange another sprig of boxwood on each ribbon and add a second lime.

Place the tips of the cones 2 inches from the ends of the ribbons as shown in the illustration.

Add additional short sprigs of boxwood for a more dimensional effect. ④

Table Decoration Created for the Peyton Randolph House

Bowl

1 antique English Worcester dessert bowl
  3 1/8 inches high x 7 7/8 inches in diameter
Plastic cut to fit the inside of the bowl
4 small red Delicious apples
24 lady apples
4 small lemons
6 limes
6-8 unshelled almonds
2-inch sprigs of balsam
2- to 3-inch sprigs of yaupon holly berries
  with the leaves removed

Dividers

2 strips of heavy plastic 3 inches wide x 15 inches
  long
2 medium oranges
4 lemons
4 limes
8 lady apples
2- to 3-inch sprigs of balsam
2-inch sprigs of yaupon holly berries with the leaves
  removed
18-20 unshelled almonds

LINE the bottom of the dessert bowl with the plastic to protect it from the fruit. Center the bowl on the table.

Fill the bowl with a mixture of red Delicious apples, lady apples, lemons, and limes. Fit the fruit together so that spaces cannot be seen.

Top the fruit with 6-8 unshelled almonds, sprigs of balsam, and 2- to 3-inch sprigs of yaupon holly berries. ①

Place the 2 strips of plastic opposite each other on the table so that they radiate from the base of the bowl toward the edges of the table.

Arrange the fruit on the plastic. To create matching designs, select pieces of fruit that are as similar in size as possible. ②

Use sprigs of balsam to pull the design together and also to conceal the plastic. Arrange the holly berries and 18-20 unshelled almonds gently to avoid dislodging the balsam. ③

Christmas Table at the George Wythe House

1 glass salver 12 inches in diameter and 7 inches high

1 glass salver 8 inches in diameter and 7 inches high

1 sweetmeat stand 13 inches high with 10 baskets and an orange cup. The orange cup is 4 ½ inches in diameter and 2 inches deep.

6 jelly glasses filled with mint jelly

7 figures

4 sweetmeat dishes

PLACE the 2 salvers in the center of the table with the smaller salver on top of the larger. Place the sweetmeat stand with its baskets and orange cup on top of the smaller salver.

Orange Cup

15-20 pieces of candied orange peel

12-15 kumquats

1 orange

Fill the orange cup with candied orange peel and kumquats. Nestle the orange in the cup. ①

Baskets

20 pieces of candied orange peel

60 sugar-coated almonds

Fill the 4 baskets with candied orange peel and the 6 baskets with sugar-coated almonds. ②

④

③

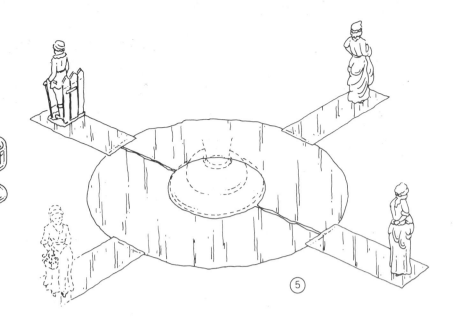

⑤

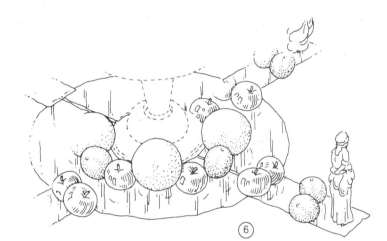

⑥

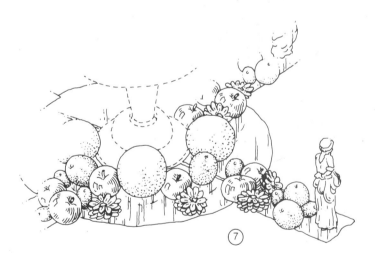

⑦

Salvers

16 candied orange slices
4 dried prunes
3 small clusters of green grapes
3-4 limes
2-3 lady apples
10-12 kumquats

Place the filled jelly glasses and 3 figures on the bottom salver. Arrange the candied orange slices and the dried prunes between the jelly glasses. ③

Arrange the 3 small clusters of green grapes and the limes on the smaller salver. Arrange the lady apples and kumquats on the grapes. ④

Table

1 circle of heavy plastic 14 inches in diameter, cut in half
4 strips of heavy plastic 2 inches wide x 6 inches long
4 small oranges
12 small limes
12 small lady apples
16 scrub pine cones with their tops cut out
16 kumquats
3-inch sprigs of boxwood
3-inch sprigs of white pine
20 unshelled almonds
2-inch sprigs of berried bayberry with the foliage removed
30-35 pieces of candied orange peel
9 marzipan strawberries
2 marzipan limes
9 marzipan apples

Cut a semicircle out of each half of the plastic. Arrange the halves around the base of the salvers so that they form a circle. Place the 4 strips of plastic so that they radiate from the base of the salvers toward the edges of the table.

Place 1 figure about 2 inches from the end of each strip of plastic. ⑤

Begin forming the design with the oranges and limes; continue with the lady apples. ⑥ Add the scrub pine cones with their tops cut out. Arrange the kumquats between the lady apples and the limes. ⑦

Use sprigs of boxwood to conceal the plastic. Add sprigs of white pine to give dimension to the design.

Continued

55

Place the unshelled almonds and the sprigs of bayberry on the arrangement gently to avoid dislodging the greens. ⑧

Finish the design by adding the sweetmeat dishes filled with candied orange peel and marzipan strawberries, limes, and apples. ⑨

The antique porcelain figures and the sweetmeat dishes are an integral part of this design. We suggest that you substitute objects d'art of your own.

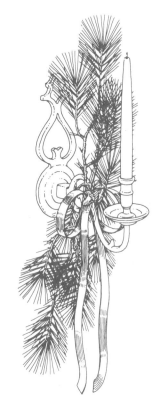

Accents

Holly Swag for Sconce

2 18-inch holly branches with berries
2 10-inch holly branches with berries
3 pieces of #22 gauge floral wire in 6-inch lengths
Wire cutters
1 yard of ⅝-inch-wide red satin ribbon
Scissors

AN overall length of 22-24 inches is in scale with most sconces.

Place 1 of the 18-inch holly branches in one direction and the other 18-inch branch in the opposite direction, overlapping the stems and concealing them behind the leaves.① Lay the 2 10-inch branches on top, stem ends overlapping, so that their overall length is 10-14 inches.② Wrap 1 wire tightly several times around the middle of the 4 branches and twist it several times in back.③ Wrap 1 wire around the 4 branches several inches above the center wire.④ Wrap another wire around the 4 branches several inches below the center wire.⑤ Cut off any excess wire. Conceal all wires with the holly leaves.

Tie the center of the swag to the arm of the sconce with the ribbon covering the wire.⑥ Tie a bow, and cut the ends of the ribbon at a slant.

NOTE: A holly swag will last 5-6 days indoors.

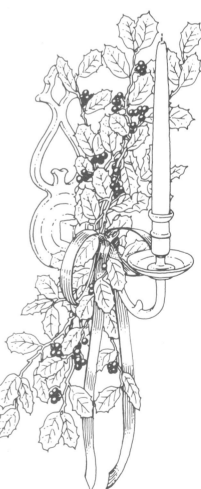

58

White Pine Swag for Sconce

2 20-inch white pine branches
2 12-inch white pine branches
3 pieces of #22 gauge floral wire in 6-inch lengths
Wire cutters
1 yard of ⅝-inch-wide red satin ribbon

AN overall length of 26-28 inches is in scale with most sconces.

Place 1 of the 20-inch white pine branches in one direction and the other 20-inch branch in the opposite direction, overlapping the stems and concealing them behind the pine needles.① Lay the 2 12-inch branches on top, stem ends overlapping, so that their overall length is 14-18 inches.② Wrap 1 wire tightly several times around the middle of the 4 branches and twist it several times in back.③ Wrap 1 wire around the 4 branches several inches above the center wire.④ Wrap another wire around the 4 branches several inches below the center wire.⑤ Cut off any excess wire. Conceal all wires with the pine needles.

Tie the center of the swag to the arm of the sconce with the ribbon, covering the wire.⑥ Tie a bow, and cut the ends of the ribbon at a slant.

NOTE: A pine swag will last 5-7 days indoors.

59

Roping

8- to 9-inch sprigs of white pine
Cord or twine
1 spool of #20 gauge floral wire
Wire cutters

FOR an illustration of white pine roping, see page 17.

Hold a bunch of 3-4 sprigs of white pine and the cord in the left hand and the spool of wire in the right.① Wrap the wire around the stems of the white pine and around the cord 4 times.② Do not cut the wire from the spool.

Assemble another bunch of 3-4 sprigs of white pine and lay it in the same direction on the first bunch on the cord several inches from the end so that it overlaps the first bunch and covers the stems.③ Twist the attached spool wire tightly around the 2 bunches 2-3 times.④ Be careful to wrap the stems only; if the needles are wrapped, it will spoil the fullness of the roping.

Keep the bunches of white pine uniform in size. To complete the roping, continue wiring bunches of white pine together, working in 1 direction.⑤

Attach the last bunch of white pine in the opposite direction. Twist the attached spool wire tightly around the last 2 bunches. Cut the wire from the spool.⑥

NOTE: Other natural materials for roping such as holly, boxwood, and white pine can be combined in random bunches.

Door Corner Accent of Holly Berries

6 12-inch holly branches with berries
6 10-inch holly branches with berries
Clippers
2 pieces of #18 gauge floral wire in 18-inch lengths
Wire cutters

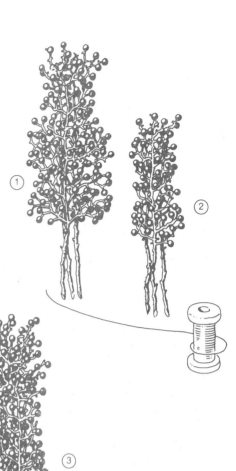

SELECT holly branches that are heavily covered with berries. Cut all of the leaves off of the holly branches with the clippers.

Bunch about 3 12-inch stems together in 1 direction.① Overlap them with 3 10-inch stems.② Wrap the wire tightly several times around the stems and twist it several times in back.③ Cut off any excess wire. Leave 4 inches of bare stems with sharp ends to insert into the roping at the corner of a doorway.

Prepare the second bunch of holly in the same manner.

NOTE: Chinaberries and rose hips may also be used as door corner accents but they should be wired on picks before inserting them into the roping.

Door Corner Accent of Lady Apples

2 pieces of #16 gauge floral wire in 22-inch lengths
16 lady apples that are uniform in size
Pliers

PUSH 1 piece of wire through the side centers of 8 lady apples and shape them into a circle.① Twist the ends of the wire together with the pliers. ②

Form a second ring in the same manner.

Use a pair of lady apple rings on top of roping in the corners of a doorway.

NOTE: A Delicious-type apple with a pointed blossom end will not lie flat and therefore is not suitable for this decoration.

62

Pomegranate Accent

1 piece of #18 gauge floral wire 18 inches in
  length
1 small pomegranate
Wire cutters
6 small magnolia leaves
Clippers
2 fern pins
15-20 2-inch sprigs of holly berries with the
  leaves removed

Push the piece of wire through the side center
of the pomegranate so that it protrudes an equal
distance on each side. Bend the wire into a "U"
shape toward the base of the pomegranate. ①
Attach the pomegranate by holding the wire ends
2 inches apart and pushing them through the
middle of the greens on the roping or wreath. ②
Twist the wires several times at the back to secure
the pomegranate. Cut off any extra wire.

Cut the stem ends off of the magnolia leaves
with the clippers. ③ Arrange the magnolia leaves
in 2 clusters of 3 leaves each. Tuck the clusters
under the right and left sides of the pomegranate
so that they radiate outward. Secure each cluster
with a fern pin. ④

Insert the holly berries around the pomegranate. ⑤

NOTE: Use this accent as a special touch on
roping, on a wreath, or at the corner of a door.

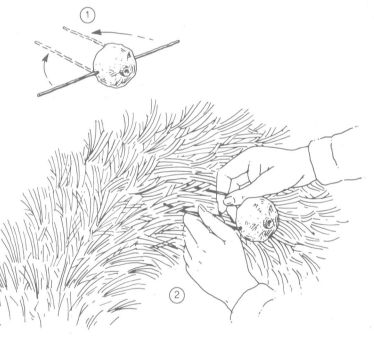

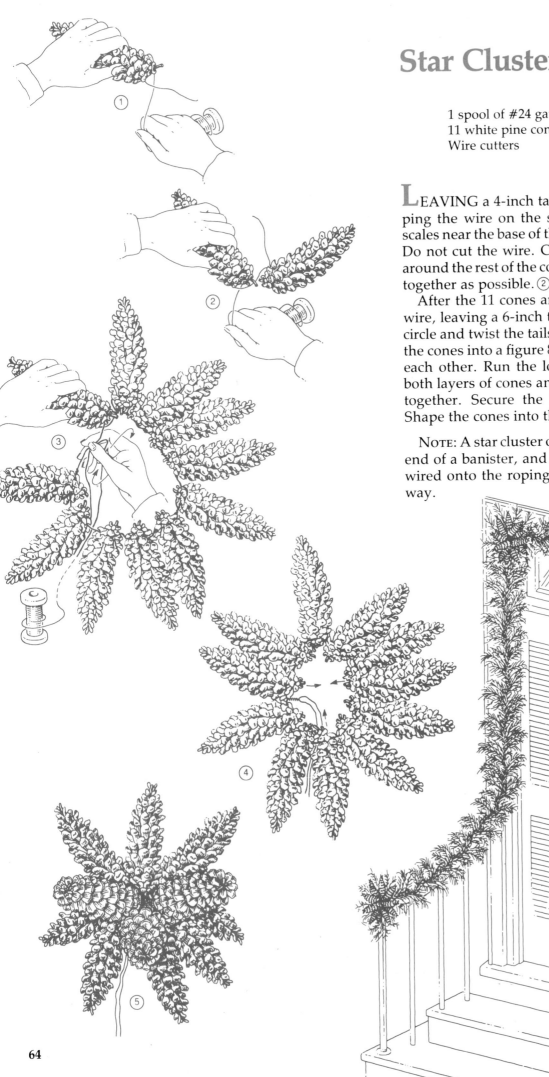

Star Cluster of Cones

1 spool of #24 gauge floral wire
11 white pine cones per cluster
Wire cutters

LEAVING a 4-inch tail of wire, begin by wrapping the wire on the spool 2 times around the scales near the base of the first white pine cone.① Do not cut the wire. Continue to wrap the wire around the rest of the cones, pulling them as close together as possible. ②

After the 11 cones are wired together, cut the wire, leaving a 6-inch tail. Form the cones into a circle and twist the tails of wire together.③ Form the cones into a figure 8 and fold the 2 loops onto each other. Run the long length of wire across both layers of cones and under the back, pulling together. Secure the 2 ends of wire again.④ Shape the cones into the star design.⑤

NOTE: A star cluster of cones may be used at the end of a banister, and matching clusters may be wired onto the roping in the corners of a doorway.

64

Cranberry Strings

1 1-pound bag of cranberries
1 darning needle
1 spool of heavy duty thread

USE only firm cranberries; discard any that are blemished or soft.

Thread the needle with a 3-foot length of heavy duty thread. Knot one end. String the cranberries lengthwise to within 3 inches of the other end. Knot the end. ①

Cranberries may be draped on kissing balls, wreaths, or Christmas trees. Use floral pins to hold them in place on kissing balls and wreaths.

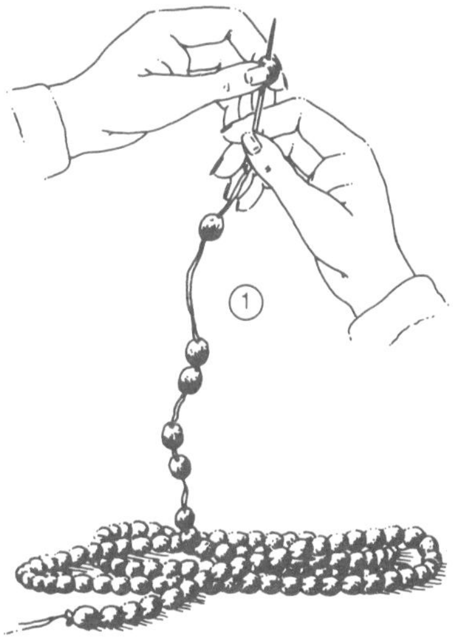

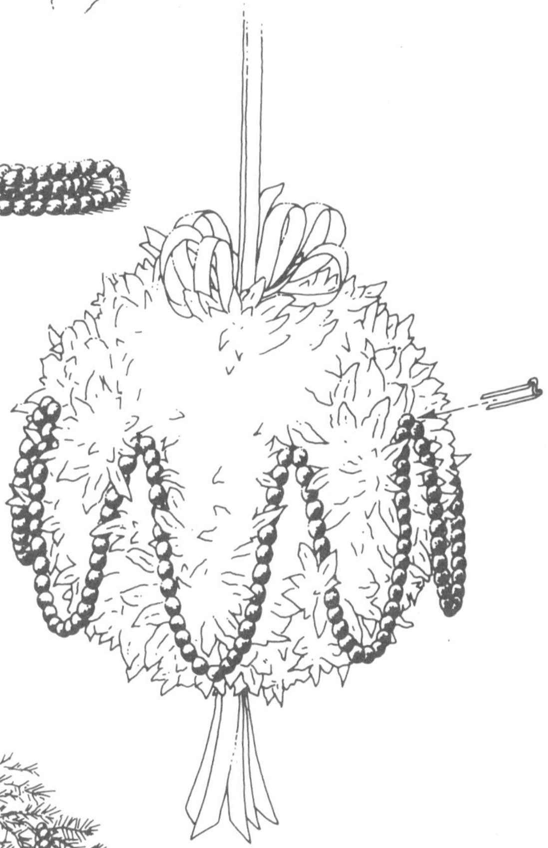

Mantel Decoration of Fruit and Natural Materials

1 block of floral foam 9 inches long x 3 inches high x 4 inches wide
1 9 inch x 4 inch green plastic floral foam holder
17 medium okra pods
21 pieces of #18 gauge floral wire in 18-inch lengths

Brown floral tape
4 medium lotus pods
9 loblolly pine cones
26 6-inch floral picks
3 medium red Delicious apples
9 lady apples
5 limes

6- to 8-inch sprigs of scrub pine with the lower needles removed
4- to 5-inch sprigs of holly with all but 2-3 of the leaves removed
4- to 5-inch sprigs of holly *or* other red berries with the leaves removed

Continued

THIS decoration will measure 26-28 inches across.

Soak the floral foam in water, insert it in the green plastic holder, and place the holder on the mantel.

Wire the okra pods as shown in the illustration. Leave twisted 6- to 9-inch wire tails. Wrap the wires with brown floral tape. Arrange the okra pods as shown in the illustration. ①

Wire the lotus pods in the same manner and wrap the wires with brown floral tape. Insert the lotus pods as shown in the illustration. ②

Wire the loblolly pine cones on 6-inch floral picks by looping the wire on the pick in and around the bottom row of scales on the cone.

Wrap the wire tightly around the floral pick several times. Insert the loblolly pine cones as shown in the illustration. ③

Impale the red Delicious apples on 6-inch floral picks and insert them toward the middle of the arrangement. ④ Keep them low to prevent the arrangement from tipping over. If it does seem unsteady, put a small wedge of paper in the front.

Impale the lady apples and limes on floral picks. ⑤ Use them to fill in the arrangement. ⑥

Fill in the design with enough sprigs of scrub pine and holly to cover the floral foam and the picks. ⑦

Tuck in the holly berries as a last touch. ⑧

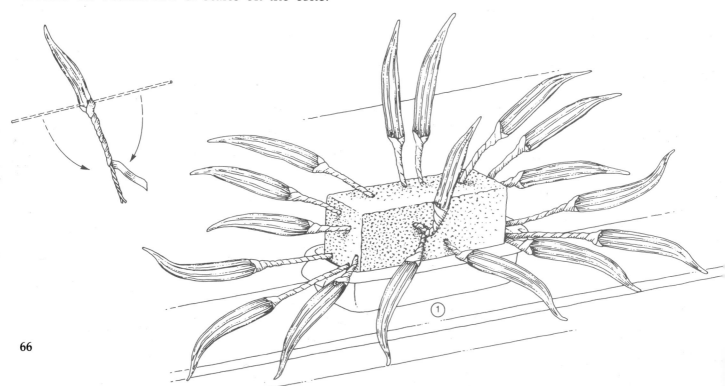

Mantel Arrangement Featuring Pineapple and Lemons

1 small pineapple
20 large lemons
12-18 floral pins (optional)
3- to 4-inch sprigs of boxwood

2 white pine cones
4 white pine cone tips

PLACE the pineapple on the mantel. It will be the center of the decoration.①

Position 4 lemons against the wall to the right of the pineapple with their ends pointing outward.② Floral pins may be used to hold the lemons together. Balance or pin a row of 3 lemons on top of the first row and a row of 2 lemons on top of the preceding row.③ Tilt 1 lemon slightly upward on top of the row of 2 lemons.④

Repeat the pyramid of lemons to the left of the pineapple.

Tuck sprigs of boxwood into any spaces between and behind the lemons, making sure the floral pins are hidden, and around the base of the pineapple.⑤

Place a pine cone at the far right and left sides of the pyramids of lemons.⑥ Place 2 pine cone tips at the base of the pineapple and 1 at the center of the base of each pyramid of lemons.⑦

NOTE: To protect the mantel, cover it with a strip of plastic. This is especially important if the lemons are pierced with floral pins.

Decorations Featuring
Herbs and Dried
and Natural Materials

Dried Herb Wreath

8 pieces of floral foam 4 inches long × 2 inches wide
   × 1 inch deep
1 10-inch wire frame with wire clasps
Pliers
6 pieces of dried yarrow with 3- to 4-inch stems ①
9 pieces of dried cockscomb with 3- to 4-inch
   stems ②
1/3-1/2 bushel basket of 3- to 4-inch sprigs of dried
   sage foliage ③
10-12 3- to 4-inch sprigs of bayberry foliage ④
8 bee balm seed heads with 3- to 4-inch stems ⑤
12-14 3- to 4-inch sprigs of dried tansy ⑥
4-6 3- to 4-inch sprigs of dried chives ⑦
8-10 3- to 4-inch sprigs of dried basil ⑧
5 3- to 4-inch sprigs of dried horehound foliage ⑨
30 3- to 4-inch pieces of white globe amaranth ⑩
16 bunches of rabbit tobacco with 3- to 4-inch
   stems ⑪
12-14 3- to 4-inch sprigs of dried marjoram ⑫
6 3- to 4-inch sprigs of dried coriander ⑬

12 dried dill seed heads with 3- to 4-inch stems ⑭
6 3- to 4-inch pieces of dried fennel ⑮
20-24 3- to 4-inch sprigs of dried lavender ⑯
8-10 3- to 4-inch sprigs of dried lemon thyme
   foliage ⑰
12-15 3- to 4-inch sprigs of dried rosemary foliage ⑱
36-40 3- to 4-inch sprigs of dried rue ⑲
18-20 3- to 4-inch pieces of blue salvia ⑳
26-30 3- to 4-inch sprigs of dried oregano ㉑
14-16 3- to 4-inch stems of multiflora rose hips ㉒
9 hot red peppers ㉓
Green floral tape
20 wooden toothpicks

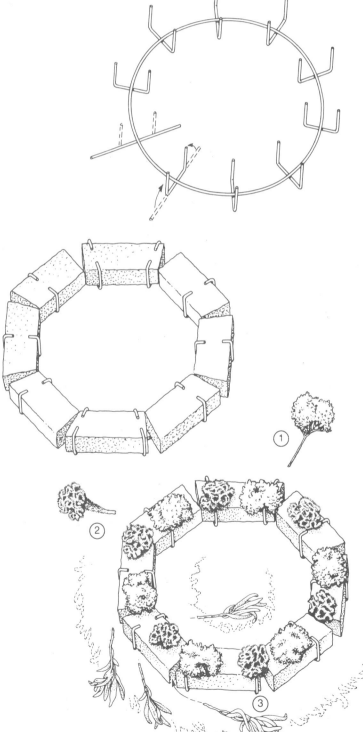

FIT the pieces of floral foam on the wire ring. Bend the wire clasps up over the pieces of floral foam to secure them.

Insert 6 pieces of yarrow equidistant from each other and down close to the floral foam. Insert 6 pieces of cockscomb close into the floral foam, centering them between the yarrow.

Cover the entire form in one direction with sprigs of dried sage, making sure that the inside and outside edges are hidden by the dried sage foliage.

With green floral tape, tape the pieces of blue salvia to toothpicks with 3-4 blooms on each toothpick. Tape the pieces of white globe amaranth to toothpicks in the same manner with 5 blooms on each toothpick. Tape the hot red peppers individually in the same manner.

Add the other dried materials, including the 3 additional pieces of cockscomb, keeping the colors and the materials distributed evenly. The larger, heavier materials should be placed down deeper in the sage. The lighter, more delicate materials should extend out from all sides to add depth, which is important in any wreath.

NOTE: A straw wreath base may be used, but more dried material will be required because it must be pinned to the frame with floral pins and dried sage crumbles easily.

An attractive wreath may be created using fewer of the dried materials.

This herb wreath should last for years and is appropriate for any season. Store it in a closed box with mothballs.

Herb Kissing Ball

1 piece of floral foam 4 1/2 inches long × 4 inches
   high × 3 1/2 inches wide
1 piece of chicken wire 17 inches × 18 inches
2 pieces of #18 gauge floral wire in 10-inch lengths
1/4 bushel of 3- to 4-inch sprigs of bayberry foliage
1/4 bushel of 3- to 4-inch sprigs of dried sage
25-30 3- to 4-inch bunches of rose hips
2 yards of red ribbon + a double length for
   hanging
2 3-inch floral picks

ENCASE the floral foam securely in the chicken wire to form a cage.① Insert 1 10-inch piece of #18 gauge floral wire down through the center of the cage. Bend the bottom of the wire into a fishhook shape. Make certain that the hook is firmly attached to the outside of the wire cage. Bend the top of the wire into a loop.② Attach the other 10-inch piece of #18 gauge floral wire to the loop. Bend the top of the second wire into a loop. Use the second piece of wire to suspend the kissing ball at a convenient working height.③

Insert 3- to 4-inch sprigs of bayberry foliage into the floral foam so that the ball is entirely covered.④ The bayberry will dry slowly and will keep its green color. Insert the 3- to 4-inch sprigs of dried sage.⑤ Insert the 3- to 4-inch bunches of rose hips.⑥

Turn the ball frequently while working on it to be sure that its shape is uniform. The finished ball should be about 8-10 inches in diameter.

To make the bow, fold the ribbon as shown in the illustration into 3 6-inch loops. Wire the bow on a floral pick.⑦ Insert the bow in the top of the kissing ball. To make the streamers, fold and cut the ribbon as shown in the illustration into 5 6-inch pieces.⑧ Wire the streamers on a floral pick. Insert the streamers into the bottom of the kissing ball. Use a double length of ribbon for hanging.⑨

NOTE: This same basic technique can be used to make a fresh boxwood kissing ball. The floral foam should first be soaked in water until it is saturated. Let the ball hang until all excess water

has dripped out. Approximately 1/4 bushel of 3- to 4-inch sprigs of boxwood is needed for a boxwood kissing ball.

Sphagnum moss encased in chicken wire can be used as a base instead of floral foam. A styrofoam ball may be used if the kissing ball is to hang for only three or four days.

A boxwood kissing ball may be decorated in many ways: drape strings of cranberries around the ball in a scallop design; add a sprig of holly at the top and bottom of the ball; add sprigs of holly or pyracantha berries at random around the ball; add small cones at random around the ball.

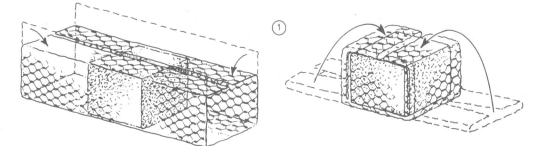

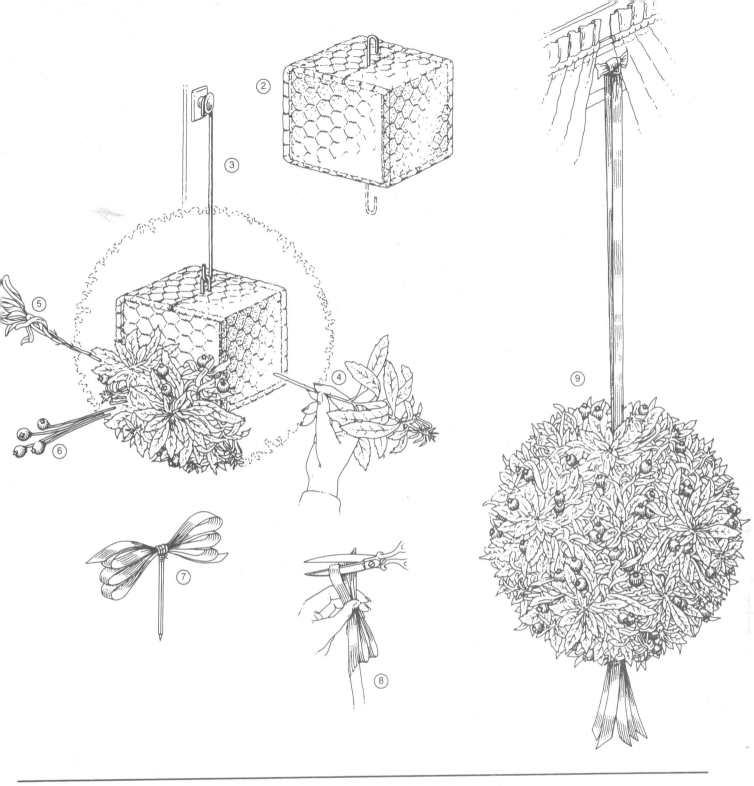

Table Decoration Designed for the Dining Room at Carter's Grove Plantation

2 pieces of galvanized clothesline wire or other very
  heavy wire in 36-inch lengths
Brown floral tape
Masking tape
123 pieces of #20 gauge floral wire in 4- to 6-inch
  lengths
Wire cutters
14-16 3- to 4-inch pieces of China fir (Cunninghamia)

10 5-inch stems of multiflora rose hips
8 Japanese iris pods with 1-inch stems or 8 pieces of
  wheat
12 white or cream strawflowers with 1-inch stems
4 hickory nut husk sections with a hole drilled in 1
  end or 4 beech leaves
6 sweet gum balls with 1-inch stems

Continued

73

8 China fir cones (*Cunninghamia*) or 8 small
  scrub pine cones
6 5-inch locust pods or 6 trumpet vine pods
8 small cockscombs with 1-inch stems or 8 red
  strawflowers or 8 staghorn sumac blooms
4 English walnuts with a hole drilled in 1 end
4 poppy pods with 2-inch stems or 4 white
  strawflowers
8 cotton bolls with 1-inch stems or 8 English
  walnuts with a hole drilled in 1 end
8 scrub pine cones
4 white pine cone tips
8 white pine cone bottom halves
8 hickory nuts with a hole drilled in 1 end
6 okra pods or 6 trumpet vine pods or 6 locust
  pods
6 loblolly pine cone bottom halves
2 6- to 8-inch pieces of cornhusks
4 chestnuts with a hole drilled in 1 end
4 trumpet vine pods or okra pods
6 white pine cones
2 6- to 8-inch pieces of cornhusks, looped
3 fresh or dried pomegranates or apples or
  gourds
Teaspoon
Small pieces of newspaper
1 piece of #18 gauge floral wire in 6-inch length
30-34 4- to 5-inch sprigs of boxwood

BEND each of the 2 pieces of clothesline wire
into an S-shaped curve as shown in the color
photograph and drawing. Wrap the pieces of
wire with brown floral tape. Mark each wire with
3 pieces of masking tape as indicated in the
diagram to show the placement of the loblolly
pine cone bottom halves. Before starting, make
sure that the pieces of wire lie flat.

Instructions for drilling and wiring nuts are
given on page 41.

Wire the pieces of plant material with 4- to
6-inch pieces of #20 gauge floral wire. Do not
wire the China fir, the rose hip stems, and the
sprigs of boxwood. Wrap the wires with brown
floral tape. Wrap the China fir and rose hip stems
with brown floral tape.

The wired materials will be attached to the main
clothesline wire by twisting the short pieces of
wire around the main wire. Trim any excess wire
and cover the ends with brown floral tape. The
stems of the China fir and the rose hips will be
attached to the main wire with brown floral tape.
Keep the larger, heavier pieces of material close to
the main wire and the lighter material to the

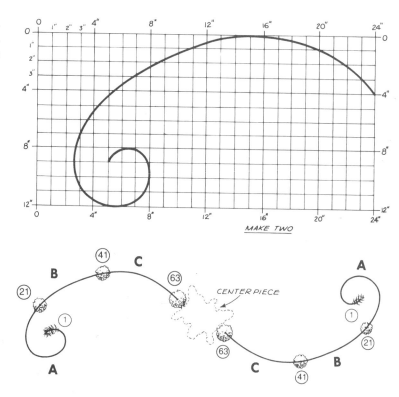

MAKE TWO

CENTER PIECE

outside, distributing the colors evenly. This construction technique enables the creation of an airy and graceful design.

A

B

C

Starting at 1 curved end, wire or tape the materials to the main wire in approximately the following order: ① 3-4 pieces of China fir, ② rose hip stem, ③ 2 Japanese iris pods, ④ 3 strawflowers bunched together, ⑤ hickory nut husk section, ⑥ sweet gum ball, ⑦ China fir cone, ⑧ locust pod, ⑨ cockscomb, ⑩ English walnut, ⑪ poppy pod, ⑫ cotton boll, ⑬ scrub pine cone, ⑭ China fir, ⑮ white pine cone tip, ⑯ white pine cone bottom half, ⑰ hickory nut, ⑱ okra pod, ⑲ rose hip stem, ⑳ China fir cone, ㉑ loblolly pine cone bottom half, ㉒ cornhusk, ㉓ scrub pine cone, ㉔ cockscomb, ㉕ cotton boll, ㉖ hickory nut, ㉗ chestnut, ㉘ white pine cone bottom half, ㉙ sweet gum ball, ㉚ trumpet vine pod, ㉛ rose hip stem, ㉜ locust pod, ㉝ China fir, ㉞ scrub

pine cone, ㉟ China fir, ㊱ white pine cone, ㊲ cotton boll, ㊳ 2 iris pods, ㊴ cockscomb, ㊵ okra pod, ㊶ loblolly pine cone bottom half, ㊷ rose hip stem, ㊸ English walnut, ㊹ 3 strawflowers bunched together, ㊺ cotton boll, ㊻ white pine cone bottom half, ㊼ locust pod, ㊽ scrub pine cone, ㊾ sweet gum ball, ㊿ white pine cone tip, 51 poppy pod, 52 rose hip stem, 53 trumpet vine pod, 54 China fir cone, 55 China fir, 56 okra pod, 57 white pine cone bottom half, 58 chestnut, 59 2 hickory nuts together, 60 hickory nut husk section, 61 cockscomb, 62 looped cornhusk, 63 loblolly pine cone bottom half.

Repeat in the same order for the other half of the curve. *Continued*

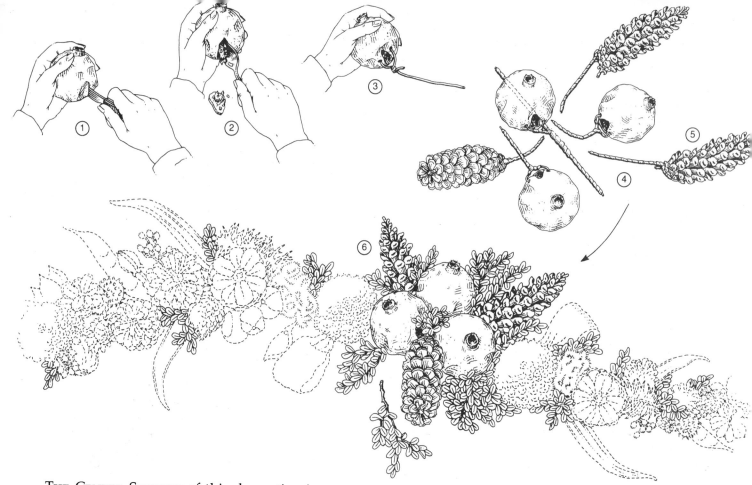

THE CENTER SECTION of this decoration is composed of 3 fresh or dried pomegranates and 3 white pine cones. If fresh pomegranates are used, hollow them out to prevent them from dripping on the table. Remove a wedge-shaped section from one side of the pomegranate large enough to insert a teaspoon.① Gently scrape the flesh and seeds loose and scoop them out.② If possible, let the pomegranates air dry for a few days. Stuff the pomegranates loosely with small pieces of newspaper. Wire the pomegranates across their openings and wrap the wires with brown floral tape.③

Wrap the 6-inch piece of #18 gauge wire with brown floral tape. Wire the pomegranates to the 6-inch piece of wire so that the openings do not show.④ Attach 3 white pine cones in between the pomegranates.⑤

When the entire design is finished and in place, tuck in sprigs of boxwood as desired.⑥

NOTE: Other natural materials may be substituted for the ones used in this decoration. It is important, however, to maintain a sense of proportion by using a variety of shapes and colors.

This decoration should keep for years if it is stored in a box with mothballs.

Garland Designed for the Mantel at Carter's Grove Plantation

1 12-inch coathanger wire *or* other heavy wire
Pliers
Brown floral tape
44-48 pieces of #20 gauge floral wire in 4- to 6-inch lengths
3 Japanese iris pods with 4-inch stems *or* 3 pieces of wheat
1 small bunch of rabbit tobacco *or* 1 white or cream strawflower
3 white or cream strawflowers with 1-inch stems

1 cluster of alder cones with 1-inch stems *or* hemlock cones *or* small pine cones
2 locust pods approximately 5 inches long *or* 2 trumpet vine pods *or* 2 okra pods
2 3-inch stems of multiflora rose hips *or* 6 small red strawflowers with 1-inch stems
2 6- to 8-inch pieces of cornhusks
15-18 acorns wired together in a cluster
1 deodara cone *or* 1 white pine cone bottom half
2 okra pods *or* 2 trumpet vine pods

1 sweet gum ball with 1-inch stem
2 4-inch pieces of China fir (Cunninghamia) or 2 beech leaves
1 white pine cone tip
3 fresh or dried pomegranates or 3 gourds
Teaspoon
Small pieces of newspaper
1 beech leaf with 1-inch stem
1 yucca pod or 1 English walnut with a hole drilled in 1 end
1 white pine cone bottom half
2 spruce cones

1 cockscomb with 1-inch stem or 1 staghorn sumac bloom
2 English walnuts with a hole drilled in 1 end
1 milkweed pod
3 cotton bolls or 3 yucca pods or 3 English walnuts with a hole drilled in 1 end
1 white pine cone
1 loblolly pine cone bottom half
1 6- to 8-inch piece of cornhusk, looped
3 hickory nut husk sections with a hole drilled in 1 end, wired together
5-7 sprigs of boxwood

ILLUSTRATED is the center garland from a mantel decoration at Carter's Grove. The design consists of five separate parts, the center garland, two swags, and a garland at each end. For the swags, clothesline wire is measured, cut, and bent into the shape and length desired, with a loop for hanging at each end. The swags may be decorated with any or all of the dried materials used in the Carter's Grove table arrangement. Follow the same techniques. The end garlands are similar to the center garland and are created in the same way.

Bend the top of the 12-inch coathanger wire into a loop with the pliers. The loop will be used to hang the garland. Wrap the entire wire with brown floral tape.

If fresh pomegranates are used, hollow them out to prevent them from dripping. Remove a wedge-shaped section from one side of the pomegranate large enough to insert a teaspoon. Gently scrape the flesh and seeds loose and scoop them out. If possible, let the pomegranates air dry for a few days. Stuff the pomegranates loosely with small pieces of newspaper. Wire the pomegranates across their openings and wrap the wires with brown floral tape.

Instructions for drilling and wiring nuts are given on page 41.

Wire the pieces of plant material with 4- to 6-inch pieces of #20 gauge floral wire. Do not wire the Japanese iris pods and the sprigs of boxwood. Wrap the wires with brown floral tape. Wrap the stems of the Japanese iris pods with brown floral tape. *Continued*

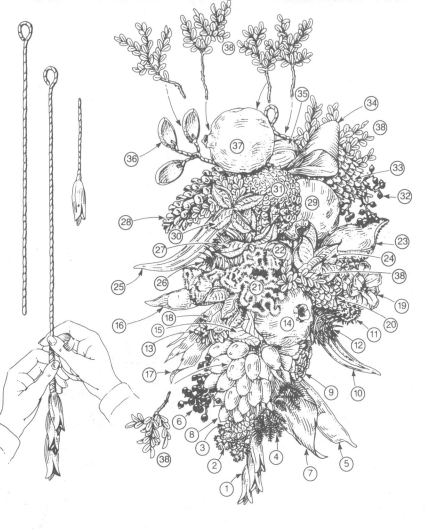

The wired materials will be attached to the main coathanger wire by twisting the short pieces of wire around the main wire. Trim any excess wire and cover the ends with brown floral tape. The stems of the Japanese iris pods will be attached to the main wire with brown floral tape.

Starting at the bottom end, wire or tape the materials to the main wire in approximately the following order: ① 3 Japanese iris pods, ② rabbit tobacco, ③ 3 strawflowers bunched together, ④ cluster of alder cones, ⑤ locust pod, ⑥ rose hip stem, ⑦ cornhusk, ⑧ cluster of acorns, ⑨ deodara cone, ⑩ okra pod, ⑪ sweet gum ball, ⑫ China fir, ⑬ white pine cone tip, ⑭ pomegranate, ⑮ beech leaf, ⑯ locust pod, ⑰ cornhusk, ⑱ yucca pod, ⑲ white pine cone bottom half, ⑳ spruce cone, ㉑ cockscomb, ㉒ English walnut, ㉓ milkweed pod, ㉔ cotton boll, ㉕ okra pod, ㉖ China fir, ㉗ cotton boll, ㉘ white pine cone, ㉙ pomegranate, ㉚ cotton boll, ㉛ loblolly pine cone bottom half, ㉜ rose hip stem, ㉝ spruce cone, ㉞ looped cornhusk, ㉟ English walnut, ㊱ 3 hickory nut husk sections, ㊲ pomegranate, ㊳ sprigs of boxwood.

Insert the sprigs of boxwood as needed after the design is finished and in place.

NOTE: This decoration should keep for years if it is stored in a box with mothballs.

Pyramid of Herbs and Fresh Fruits

1 16-inch square of chicken wire
Ruler
Heavy gloves
Wire cutters
Sphagnum moss
1 3-inch orchid tube
Urn-shaped container *or* compote *or* pedestal cake stand
18-20 3- to 4-inch sprigs of Jerusalem sage *or* any sage
7 white pine cones
Clippers

66-74 3-inch floral picks
8 empty cotton bolls
6 sweet gum balls
10-12 small bunches of green grapes
4 small dried gourds
24-28 pieces of #18 gauge floral wire in 3-inch lengths
6 lady apples
20-24 yellow and cream strawflowers
14-18 kumquats

8-10 hickory nuts with a hole drilled in 1 end
8-10 small pieces of yarrow with 3-inch stems
14-16 3-inch sprigs of berried bayberry with the leaves removed
12-14 3- to 4-inch pieces of bittersweet with 3-inch stems
35-40 2- to 3-inch sprigs of white pine
7 poppy pods with 3-inch stems

MEASURE 4 inches from the left edge and put a mark ① as shown in the illustration. This will be the top of the cone. Wear heavy gloves to protect hands from the sharp wire. Bend the chicken wire into a cone shape. Start with the right hand corner ② of the marked side and roll it over to ③ 12 inches from ① as shown in the illustration. The diameter of the cone will measure 7 inches and the sides 12 inches. Fold the remaining top portion ④ over and bend the cut portions so that they

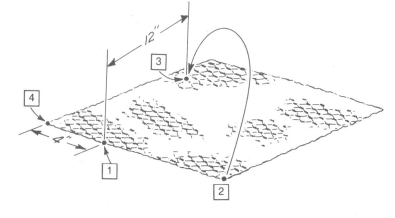

hook the cone together. Measure 12 inches from the top and trim off the excess wire so that the cone will stand straight. ①

Soak the sphagnum moss in water. Squeeze out excess moisture. Stuff the cone firmly with the damp sphagnum moss.

Cut off 1 inch of chicken wire at the top of the cone and insert the orchid tube filled with water. ②

Place the cone in an urn-shaped container or on a base. The sphagnum moss will be damp.

Insert several pieces of sage into the arrangement at random. ③

Cut the white pine cones in half with the clippers. Wire the cones on 3-inch floral picks by looping the wire on the pick in and around the bottom row of scales on the cone. Wrap the wire tightly around the floral pick several times. ④

Wire the cotton bolls on 3-inch floral picks by wrapping the wire on the pick around the stems tightly several times. Bring the wire below the stem and wrap it around the floral pick several times. ⑤

Wire the sweet gum balls ⑥ and small bunches of green grapes in the same manner. ⑦

Impale the gourds on 3-inch pieces of #18 gauge floral wire. ⑧

Impale the lady apples on 3-inch floral picks. ⑨

Continued

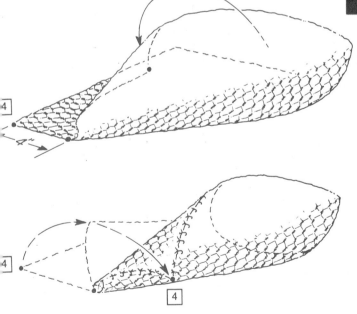

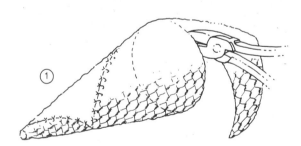

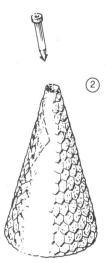

Impale the strawflowers on 3-inch pieces of #18 gauge floral wire. ⑩

Impale the kumquats on 3-inch floral picks. ⑪

Instructions for drilling and wiring the hickory nuts ⑫ are given on page 41.

The stems of the yarrow, ⑬ bayberry, ⑭ bittersweet, ⑮ sprigs of white pine, ⑯ and poppy pods ⑰ will be inserted directly into the arrangement.

Insert the plant materials evenly throughout the arrangement. Place more of the larger, heavier materials first and nearer the bottom for balance. Any mixture of fruit and dried materials can be used. It is important to keep the design in scale, to use a variety of colors and textures, and to distribute the colors evenly throughout the design.

Save the prettiest piece of sage to insert in the orchid tube in the top of the pyramid.

NOTE: Continue to keep the sphagnum moss damp in order to prolong the life of the greens.

555   740

80